Life Lessons from a Ranch Horse

Also by Mark Rashid

Horses Never Lie:
The Heart of Passive Leadership

A Good Horse Is Never a Bad Color

Considering the Horse:
Tales of Problems Solved and Lessons Learned

Life Lessons from a Ranch Horse

6 Fundamentals of Training Horses—and Yourself

Mark Rashid

Foreword by Harry Whitney

Skyhorse Publishing

Skyhorse Publishing books may be purchased in bulk at special discounts for sales promotion, corporate gifts, fund-raising, or educational purposes. Special editions can also be created to specifications. For details, contact the Special Sales Department, Skyhorse Publishing, 307 West 36th Street, 11th Floor, New York, NY 10018 or info@skyhorsepublishing.com.

Skyhorse® and Skyhorse Publishing® are registered trademarks of Skyhorse Publishing, Inc.®, a Delaware corporation.

Visit our website at www.skyhorsepublishing.com.

10 9 8 7 6 5 4 3

Library of Congress Cataloging-in-Publication Data

Rashid, Mark.
  Life lessons from a ranch horse / Mark Rashid ; with a new afterword by the author, foreword by Harry Whitney.
    pages cm
  ISBN 978-1-5107-5090-6 (pbk. : alk. paper)
  1. Horses -- Training -- Colorado -- Anecdotes. 2. Horses -- Behavior -- Colorado -- Anecdotes. 3. Rashid, Mark. 4. Horse trainers -- Colorado -- Anecdotes. 5. Human-animal communication -- Colorado --Anecdotes.
  SF287.R283 2011
  636.1/0835 23
                        16777378

Cover design by Tom Lau
Cover image credit: iStockphoto.com

Print ISBN: 978-1-5107-5090-6
Ebook ISBN: 978-1-62873-097-5

Printed in China

Contents

Foreword

I WAS TALKING TO Mark Rashid a few days ago. In among a whole series of stories, it came to light that he was writing yet another book. Now most of us could put all we have to say of any value on top of the eraser of this pencil I'm writing with. So, after three books, what more could Mark have to say?

I was introduced to Mark through his books. A mutual friend read *Considering the Horse* and said I had to read it. As soon as I did, I liked the man I saw through these stories. Can't help but like a good storyteller.

Then came book two, *A Good Horse Is Never a Bad Color*, and more good stories. But then, there was maybe something more than just a storyteller here, because in each story was a message to be learned about horses and people living in the same world. So now he was not only a storyteller, but sort of a friend, too. Even before meeting him, I considered Mark a friend who cares enough to tell a story we might learn from.

Then I met my "friend" face to face and saw him work with students and their horses. I watched and realized that this storyteller was a wonderful teacher, taking time to help people understand their horses and to help them learn how to find the try. That's when I met the horseman in Mark. As he worked to help people, I saw him searched for that little try in the horse—the one that keeps the horse from getting discouraged and allows it to search for what Mark wants and maybe even want to be around him.

Then came another book, *Horses Never Lie*. This time I could recognize the writer in Mark. To put stories in print is one thing, but to bring together real-life situations with a common theme to help us get the point takes a good writer.

In this book, *Life Lessons from a Ranch Horse*, I've met yet another side of Mark. Or is it? Maybe it's what makes all the other parts of Mark shine through. For in this book, I see what a thinker Mark is. Here he writes stories of his horse friend, Buck, and what a better teacher and horseman he is because of Buck. Now, many of us could experience the same things and not give it another thought, but not Mark.

As you read this book, consider how much Mark has thought about these things. Maybe that's why Buck didn't give up trying to teach Mark. He knew Mark was thinking and just needed time.

But do we take the time to think on similar things? Through this book, I believe Mark is trying to get us to see how much a horse can teach us, as well as share the lessons he learned. But is Mark also trying to get us thinking? Thinking about what our horses could teach us. Thinking about how much thought can go into an important lesson. Thinking about how much our horses just might be thinking themselves. It seems to me all the great horsemen I've been around are real thinkers.

So, Mark, thank you for thinking. Thinking about how people might best enjoy a story. Thinking hard about how to teach us by making the point of the story clear. Thinking about how to explain what you learned from horses to help us all to become better horsemen. Thinking about how you approach and treat others, so that they're not just students but feel like friends. Thinking about writing more books, since they keep getting better and we need them.

So back to my question. What more could Mark have to say? This book proves there is plenty. As you read this book, I hope you embark on a journey of thinking. So, read it, enjoy it, THINK!

Harry Whitney

Preface

MANY YEARS AGO I had the opportunity to meet a great singer/songwriter from West Virginia named Larry Groce. Some folks may remember Larry from the 1970s when he had a hit song titled "Junk Food Junkie," from an album (remember albums?) of the same name. At the time I was playing guitar in a bluegrass band, and we just happened to play a number of songs from Larry's album.

A few months after meeting Larry, I called him to ask if he'd like to come to our area and do a show, which he said he'd be happy to do. I mentioned that our band knew just about every song from that album, and we played them nearly note for note the way he'd recorded them. At that time, he was performing without a band when he traveled, so I told him we'd be happy to be his band for the show. There was a brief silence on the other end of the line.

Then, almost apologetically, he said, "Well, actually, Mark, I don't really play those songs very much anymore."

"You don't?" I replied in surprise.

"No," he said. "That record is over ten years old and I'm kind of on to other things now."

"But they're such great songs," I said.

"Yes, they are," he said. "But there are other great songs out there, too."

I sat holding the phone, somewhat flabbergasted. What did he mean he was on to other things? What did he mean there were other great songs? Our band had just begun to know his music, only to find that he was no longer playing it. What a shock!

I had a hard time understanding why anybody would want to relinquish something so wonderful, just leaving it behind and moving on.

The night of the show I finally understood why. Larry had called back a few days later to say he'd like to do some of the old songs with our band, after all. We opened the show with him, performing five or six songs from the album, and as promised, we did them note for note, and they did indeed sound just like the record. Then we left the stage, and Larry did a set of music alone.

Armed with only his new music and his guitar to accompany him, Larry brought the house down. The reason he'd moved on to other things was clear to me—he wanted to get better at his music. And he most certainly had. The old songs were great, and he performed them wonderfully. But the new stuff was even better, and so was he.

Larry hadn't abandoned his old music or left his old music behind. He had simply taken it with him as he moved forward. It was an indication of someone who wasn't satisfied with the status quo, even though it had gotten him where he was. It was the sign of someone in search of mastering his craft.

The problem is, when someone goes in search of mastery, people around him or her can suddenly feel left behind. I know that's how I felt when Larry first told me he'd gone on to other music.

I wanted to grab hold of him and say, "No, wait! I just now found your *old* music! I'm just starting to understand how to play it! Don't leave now! I may not like the new stuff. Or what's worse, I may like it more! Then I'm going to have to change, too. If you don't change, I won't have to either and that would be much easier on me."

Well, oddly enough, I'm finding myself in a situation similar to Larry's. In September 1992, I began writing my first book, *Considering the Horse: Tales of Problems Solved and Lessons Learned*. It was a great experience because the process of writing triggered hundreds of wonderful childhood memories that had been packed away in a musty old trunk somewhere in the attic of my subconscious. It was my first attempt at writing a book and a great opportunity to share some of my experiences—both good and bad—of working with horses.

My main goal in writing the book was to pass along training information without putting it in a "how-to" format. After all, I have a hard time reading step-by-step, how-to books, so I sure wasn't going to be able to write one. Instead of the typical format, I chose an anecdotal style. Much to everyone's surprise (mine included), the format of *Considering the Horse* seemed to strike a chord with readers and my book took off.

We had so much positive feedback on *Considering the Horse* that I was soon asked to write a follow-up book. A year or so later, *A Good Horse is Never a Bad Color* was released. It was written using the same format, although it covered different subject matter and it, too, was surprisingly well received.

Very soon after the second book came out, however, I just sort of settled back into ranching with the idea that my book-writing days were over. After all, I never really considered myself a writer in the first place, and if the truth were known, I didn't think I had anything else to say.

A few years passed and I'd slowly gotten away from ranching and started doing clinics. In some of my clinics, I began talking about a training idea I'd been working on for years, which I called "passive leadership." Put simply, it is the idea of handling and working with horses by becoming a trusted leader that the horse will choose to follow, as opposed to being an "alpha" leader that generally forces his leadership on other horses.

Evidently, the idea created a stir in some circles of the horse community and was generally misunderstood, because I used the words "passive" and "leadership" together. After all, how can one be passive and still be a leader? At any rate, soon afterward, I wrote what I truly thought would be my final book, *Horses Never Lie: The Heart of Passive Leadership*.

In *Horses Never Lie*, I remember making a conscious effort to step out of the shadow created by my first two books. They were more or less snapshots of where I'd been in my work with horses. Mostly they were written in past tense and were about circumstances and ideas that had gotten me where I was. They weren't necessarily where I was going. In fact, by the time I wrote *Horses Never Lie*, I was already working on ways of refining and, in some cases, even changing some of the methods I'd talked about in *Considering the Horse*.

Horses Never Lie also marked a subtle change in my writing style, if you will. While there are still plenty of anecdotes in the book, I was more to the point in terms of passing along my ideas. Since I felt at the time that *Horses Never Lie* would be my last book, I felt an urgency to be sure the point of the book was clearly made. I spent less time talking about the past and more time talking about the present. In short, I suppose it could be said that *Horses Never Lie* brought everyone up-to-date on where I was with my horsemanship.

Many years have now passed since I first began writing *Considering the Horse*. During that time, I have slowly made changes in my life, particularly when it comes to the way I deal with horses, but also in the ways I deal with people. I suppose an argument could be made that I've been working on trying to master my craft, a goal I know I'll probably never achieve. I've realized that, in order for me to search for mastery, some things I did in the past have to improve, some have to stay the same, and some have to be set aside.

I see this book, *Life Lessons from a Ranch Horse*, as the next step in that process. It is a sort of documentation of the fifteen years I spent with Buck, my old horse, who during that time had gently been nudging me toward a better way to go through life. Honestly, I'm not sure if he did it by accident or by design, but one thing is sure . . . he most certainly became the catalyst for my search for growth, both professionally and personally. He made me realize I wasn't going to be able to get better in my work with horses unless I first improved other things in my life.

My hope is that you enjoy reading this book as much as I've enjoyed writing it. While it does, in one sense, mark the end of a great partnership between Buck and me, it also marks a whole new beginning for both of us. For him, it's retirement and some well-deserved time off. For me, I once again find myself starting anew in a number of different areas in my life. Hopefully, this time—thanks to the lessons I've learned from Buck—I'm a little better prepared for what's in store, even though right now I'm not exactly sure what that is.

—M. R.

Life Lessons from a Ranch Horse

Introduction

SOMETIME BACK, a friend introduced me to an interesting idea. She referred to it as "The Myth of Er." Now, according to my friend, this particular story is very old and dates back to the time of Plato, perhaps even further.

Intrigued, I researched the myth and found the idea has actually been bouncing around in various cultures for hundreds of centuries. The Myth of Er has a variety of names, depending on the culture, but with the exception of a few minor details, the story is pretty much the same.

The myth says that we are all given a soul prior to coming to Earth. Before we're born for the first time, we are given the ultimate purpose for the soul—to become a wise and kind spirit, full of life and knowledge that can be passed on and improved on with each life we live. Then we're asked to choose a task to work on during the life that we are about to embark upon. The task we choose will help fulfill our soul's ultimate purpose.

After choosing the task, we are asked to choose all the aspects of our life, including the family we will be born into, the friends and acquaintances we wish to come in contact with during the life, the paths we will encounter, and even the animals we will live and work with. Once all of this has been decided, then and only did are we born into this world to begin our journey. The only thing—and this is the kicker—is that when we're born, we forget the entire process we just went through.

As we go through the life, we're faced with the outcomes of all the choices we made prior to our birth. Some are difficult to face, some are not. But all are designed to help us achieve the task we chose for that particular life. We travel through the life, and eventually we pass away. When we die, our soul returns to where it started.

Once there, our soul's memory is regained and we get to assess how we did in the life we just lived. Did we complete our task? If not, we can choose to come back in another life and try again, following the same rules, if you will. If we completed the task, we choose a different life and move on to the next task. But each time we are born, we forget what we went through in our previous lives, as well as the choices we made for our soul.

ACCORDING TO THE MYTH, it takes the soul thousands of lifetimes to become perfect. And here's where the myth gets a little foggy. Depending on the culture, different things can happen to the soul once it becomes perfect. Some Asian cultures, for instance, send the soul continually back into the same family all throughout its journey, even after it has become perfect. This is why some folks in those cultures treat their children so well—they just may end up coming back as their children's children!

I have a little different theory about what happens once a soul finally becomes perfect. I think the perfect soul is given a chance to come back as a teacher for all those individuals still working their way through their tasks. But the catch is that this time they come back as an animal or insect.

Now of course I don't have any proof to back this theory up, but if you think about it, cats might be here to help us learn to take life less seriously. Houseflies may be here to teach us patience, and ants to help teach us how to work together. Our dogs might be here to help teach us how to have fun chasing our own tails. In fact, if we look hard enough, I'll bet we can learn something positive from just about every living thing on the planet.

AND THAT BRINGS ME TO BUCK, the horse you'll be reading about in this book. A friend gave me Buck when he was seven years old, back in 1986. At the time, he'd had minimal handling. To be honest, I wasn't real crazy about starting a horse that old, but I figured, what the heck, a free horse is a free horse. In 1986 I was just starting to gain something of a reputation as a horse trainer who worked mostly with problem horses, although I was still primarily doing ranch work of one kind or another. A big, stout horse like Buck, if he worked out, would more than likely fit right into my program, so I was willing to take a chance on him.

Now you may want to read the final sentence of that paragraph again, because it'll give you a pretty good idea of my mindset when Buck and I began working together. I just assumed, like most horse people would, that I was the one who'd be doing the teaching, and he'd be the one doing the learning. And, for a while, that was true. But only for a short while. Very soon after we started working together, I began to understand that this time things were going to be different . . . because Buck was different.

I have to admit, as you will see, it took me a while to get out of my own way. But when I finally did, I saw it was me who was going to be doing the learning, not him. As the years passed and my attitude about my role slowly changed, I came to understand that I was in the presence of a truly great teacher, one who seemed to possess the wisdom of the ages. He was a teacher who ultimately became a great friend and partner. Maybe it was all in some big plan. Maybe it was just coincidence. But either way, I know for a fact that I am far better off for having known him than I would be had I not.

So this is our story. As you read, maybe you'll begin to see why I feel Buck may have carried the wisdom of the ages into our relationship . . . that he was a perfect soul that chose to be here to help me learn.

But also remember, as you read, it's only a theory. I could be wrong.

PART ONE

Lessons

School Starts

I HAD JUST FED OUR four horses, three in the corral and one in the barn, and the one in the barn wasn't eating. A horse not eating at feeding time is almost always something to be concerned about, and if it were any other horse, I might have been alarmed.

The other horses were already pinning their ears, squealing, and running each other off the three piles of hay, one for each horse. As was their ritual, for the next five minutes or so they'd play a sort of musical chairs with the piles, moving each time the smallest one of the bunch—a little 14.2-hand, line-back dun gelding named Tuff—decided he needed some hay from a different pile. With ears pinned, he would head over to the closest pile and chase off Red, a 16-hand sorrel gelding that dwarfed Tuff. Red would, in turn, pin his ears at Quincy, a 15-hand gelding eating quietly at the third pile, sending him over to the pile Tuff had abandoned at the beginning. They'd all settle back down until Tuff decided to move to the next pile, starting the whole thing over.

While it was fun watching those three sort out their eating arrangements for the evening meal, it was the gelding in the barn that had my attention. He was an old horse, Buck. At twenty-three years old, he was beginning to show his age. Only a few months earlier, I had retired him from ranch work and given him to my youngest son, Aaron.

I'd recently taken Buck off the winter pasture, because he wasn't faring as well as I liked. Although he wasn't really thin, it was obvious that he wasn't doing as well as the others on the pasture. He was a hard-keeper to begin with, and any time he started to lose weight it raised a red flag for me. I brought Buck home so I could supplement his diet and maybe get him to put on a few pounds.

Buck stood in his run just outside the barn and stared at me. He watched my every move, occasionally shifting his weight from one hind leg to the other. Even though I'd just put his nightly share of pellets in his stall, he completely ignored them, a behavior that would worry most folks. A horse not eating, especially his extra feed, usually meant something serious was going on, colic maybe. But I could tell that Buck wasn't sick. He was just trying to tell me something.

I was pretty busy at the time and tried to ignore him as I went about my chores. But after all the years we'd been together, I knew when he got this way, it would be impossible to ignore him for long. I turned and looked at him.

"What?" I asked.

As if answering, he nonchalantly turned his head and looked into his stall. I walked over to the run, reached through the panels, and stroked his neck. He kept his head turned, and even though I could barely see his left eye, the one closest to me, I saw that he was looking at me.

Fine. At least I knew that whatever it was he wanted must be in his stall. Probably something with his pellets, I thought. I put my rake down, walked around the corner and into the barn, opened the metal sliding door to his stall, and went in. Buck met me in the stall. I checked the pellets for foreign objects; there weren't any. I picked them up, smelled them, and even tasted them to see if they were okay; they were. I checked to make sure he had plenty of clean water; he did.

He stood looking at me. I looked around in the stall but couldn't see anything out of the ordinary, so I petted him on his head and left the stall. He snorted loudly and shook his head. I returned and looked at him through the door. He quietly turned and looked out at the horses in the corral playing musical hay piles. Again, even with his head turned, I could see that he was looking at me.

Okay, so now I knew that he wanted something he didn't have, but the others did, and it had something to do with his stall. Whatever it was, it was more important to him that the two scoops of pellets in his feeder. I knew this because, over our years together, in thousands of situations, Buck had spent a great deal of time trying to train me to listen to what he had to say. With the patience of a saint, he had presented ideas that I'd never have thought possible for any animal other than a human to have.

THE FIRST TIME Buck tried to get me to listen to him, it was to help me understand how horses do things. It happened about a year after we started working together. He was seven years old at that time.

We were working a roundup I'd helped with for many years. Like usual, we were helping a friend gather his herd of about 120 horses from twenty-five hundred acres of land. Buck and I were alone when we'd come upon thirty head up in the rocks above a small mountain valley. We successfully worked them down into the valley, and our next moves were to bring them down a draw, across a meadow about a mile in length, through a tunnel that ran under the highway, and finally into the large catch pen.

The only problem was that Buck and I ended up between the horses and the draw on the south end of the valley we needed them to go down. We would have to get around them to the north in order to drive them to the draw. This was a precarious situation, because one wrong move on my part and I could end up scattering the herd to the far ends of the pasture. On top of that, just out of sight in the trees at the north end of the valley, there was an open gate that led to another five hundred acres—and I definitely did not want them getting to that five hundred.

Buck and I slowly started to make our way around the herd, giving them a wide berth, so as not to alarm them. We were nearly all the way past the herd, and everything was going well, when I noticed the horses begin to watch us pretty carefully. Even though we were moving slowly, they started to mill around. A few of them even turned and headed toward the line of trees to the north, right where the open gate was. They weren't moving all that fast, but in my mind's eye I could see them breaking into a lope and taking the rest of the herd with them.

Wanting to get out ahead of them and stay ahead of them, I urged Buck to pick up a little jog trot. Much to my surprise, he refused. As far as I could remember, this was the first time he had refused to do anything I asked of him. I asked again, and again he refused, maintaining his slow, steady walk.

With a quick glance at the herd, I could see that a couple more horses had joined the ones already on the move. I quickly began trying to figure out why Buck's wasn't responding. We hadn't been working that long, only about an hour, and he'd been walking the majority of that time, so I knew he couldn't be tired. I turned around in the saddle and glanced back at Buck's tail to see if he needed—how can I say this delicately?—a rest stop. But that wasn't it, either.

Nope, for some strange reason he simply wasn't doing what I was asking him to do, and I didn't like it. I nudged him harder with my heel, and he swished his tail defiantly. The rest of the herd had joined the others on their trek northward, albeit at a lazy walk. I nudged him again; he responded with a tail swish and a head shake.

We'd traveled a short distance farther when I looked over to see that the herd had all but stopped. The horses had even dropped their heads to graze a bit. Instead of relaxing, I saw this as our chance to put some space between us and the herd and close off the north end. I nudged Buck again and again he refused, this time blowing hard through his nose.

It was obvious to me he couldn't see the urgency in the situation, and I was beginning to get annoyed with his refusals. Meanwhile, the horses had raised their heads and haltingly begun to move north once again. Finally, in what I can only call a fit of aggravation, I just blapped Buck hard with both heels. By this time he was just as aggravated with me as I was with him, and his aggravation came out in a jumping transition to a fast lope.

There, I thought. Finally he's doing what I want. And none too soon, because just as he jumped into a lope, the herd woke up, hesitated for just a second, and then broke as fast as they could go toward the north end of the valley. Suddenly, and I suppose not surprisingly, we found ourselves in a major foot race. It was us against thirty head of pretty fresh pasture horses, and we were all heading for the same place. Buck and I were jumping rocks and sage, dodging gopher holes, and leaping over small puddles from the previous night's rain. The herd, tails in the air and manes in the wind, were running for all they were worth, some whinnying wildly as they went.

We reached the woods going about as fast as Buck could run, and we were only about fifty yards ahead of the herd. A quick glance back over my shoulder showed the herd was gaining fast. What was worse was that we were having to dodge trees and avoid low-hanging branches, while they were on a narrow, unobstructed path that led straight through the gate and into the five hundred, now only about 120 yards in front of us.

They were flying down the path, and I knew it was going to be close, maybe too close. I urge Buck to move faster, but instead, he slowed down ever so slightly. That one hesitation was enough to let the herd shoot past us and right though the gate. Buck continued to slow from an all-out gallop, to a slow lope, to a trot, and finally to a walk. I watched helplessly as the herd disappeared into the trees and rocks of the five hundred, running just as fast as their feet could carry them.

I REMEMBER SEEING A cartoon once. It was of two horses standing side by side, both wearing saddles. One horse was looking at the other with a disgusted look on his face, and a caption read, "If my cowboy doesn't start listening to me, I'm bound to get a bad reputation."

I'm as sure as I can be that that was exactly what Buck was thinking as we stood there listening to the hoof beats of the herd fade into the distance. As for me, all I could think of at that time was how much work my horse had just caused me. Had he just gone faster when I asked him to in the first place, I reasoned, we would have no doubt had the herd in the catch pen by now. Instead, we would spend the next two-and-a-half hours searching for, gathering, and then bringing the herd back through the gate and into the small valley we'd just come from.

The nice thing about having that much time on your hands is that it gives you the opportunity to think. Now, as I said, most of my initial thoughts were of how mad I was that Buck hadn't responded when I asked him to. And that, it was my feeling, was why we were in the mess we were in. I have to admit those pretty much remained my thoughts for the next half-hour or so. In fact, I would have probably continued thinking that way had it not been for one simple thing. It doesn't seem like much now, I suppose, but at the time it turned out to be very humbling.

While I was sitting there on Buck's back, mentally beating him up for not doing what I asked, when I asked it, I noticed that he was simply going about his business, just as he had before the foot race. Not only was he going about his business, but he was doing it very thoughtfully. He was stepping carefully over rocks and downed timber. He was slowly traversing the draw and finding the safest way to the bottom. He would stop when something didn't look right to him, then turn and choose another, more prudent direction. Every once in a while he would prick his ears in a certain direction, telling me exactly where the herd was.

In short, while I was feeling sorry for myself and stewing about my horse, he had already gone back to work, pretty much without me and, indeed, in spite of me. Not only that, but he was taking care of me while he was doing it!

As I said, once I came to my senses and realized what was happening, I found it to be very humbling indeed. However, there was another lesson that I believe he tried to teach me that day that I had missed completely. Unfortunately, that particular lesson wouldn't become clear for quite some time.

FOLLOWING THE INCIDENT in the valley, Buck's apparent refusal problem just seemed to disappear. In fact, even during the rest of that day, he went right back to being just as responsive as he'd always been. His good behavior continued until about three months later, when a horse that was having a great deal of trouble leading was brought to me for help. As it turned out, he didn't really lead at all.

I had already spent some time with the young gelding in the round pen doing ground work, which he did pretty well. He even led pretty well in the pen. However, as soon as I started to lead him anywhere outside the pen, he took a few steps and locked up. I had worked with him from the ground for a couple of days with limited success, so I decided to pony the youngster off Buck. That would give me more options in terms of how I could work him. More importantly, if he got to pulling back or jerking on the end of the rope, I could just dally up and let him work against Buck instead of working against me.

The next day I took the colt and Buck to the big arena. I got up on Buck and, with the youngster's lead rope in hand, asked Buck to walk forward. Without even taking the slack out of the rope, the young gelding quietly walked next to Buck like he'd been doing it all his life. He made no trouble whatsoever. We made one uneventful lap around the arena, and things were going so well that I thought maybe all the ground work I'd done over the past couple of days had actually made a difference. Just as I was getting ready to pat myself on the back for a job well done, we passed the gate that we'd come through much as I'd hoped.

We had walked about five feet past the gate when the youngster planted his feet and refused to go any farther. Buck kept walking and very quickly the slack in the rope disappeared. Before we got to the end of the rope, however, I took a quick dally so that the pull from the rope would be on the saddle horn and not on me. As the rope put tension on the saddle horn, I could feel Buck shoulder into the pressure. It felt like we were trying to pull a tank out of the mud. I turned around to look at the youngster and saw him leaning backward with all his might, the lead rope tight as a fiddle string and his halter stretched out about as far as it could go. I could see the whites of his eyes. His nostrils flared and his lips were tight.

I asked Buck to stop, which he did without releasing the pressure. I had a pretty good idea that continuing forward might not be the most productive thing at that point. Even if the colt gave in and came forward, he would probably come in a gigantic leap, endangering all three of us. I decided to try to break his feet loose in another way. So I turned Buck to the right and, while keeping some tension in the rope, went back around the youngster's right side, ending with Buck facing north and the colt facing south. I continued to ask Buck to move forward until the youngster's head was turned to the point where it was facing the same direction as Buck and I, although his body still had not moved.

Basically, we were trying to get the youngster so far off balance that he would pretty much have to move his feet in order to regain his balance. Once he moved, we could direct him and hopefully get him leading again.

The problem was that once we got the youngster into that position, Buck just stopped. I urged him forward, squeezing him with my heels, but he refused, acting as if he didn't feel me. I asked again, but Buck didn't respond. The young horse appeared to be teetering, ready to take the next step, and I felt all we needed to do was give him just a little more encouragement to get the movement we were looking for. I asked again for some movement from Buck, and he acted as if I weren't even there.

Finally I just jabbed Buck with my heels, and he responded by just barely offering some forward movement. Much to my surprise, Buck leaning forward and putting that small amount of additional pressure on the rope was all it took for the young horse to lose his mind completely. The youngster also lost his balance and moved his feet—as I had originally hoped he would—but not at all in the way I expected. Suddenly I had an explosive ball of energy locked to my saddle horn by an eight-foot lead rope. It felt like we'd hooked a nine-hundred-pound marlin that wasn't very happy about being caught.

Well, needless to say, things got a little western for a few minutes, and by the time the dust cleared, I was happy to see that everyone was all right. We took a few minutes to regroup and were able to continue on, albeit a little slower and a whole lot more cautiously. The young gelding overcame his difficulty with leading in a relatively short period of time, and things progressed pretty smoothly from that point forward.

Even though everything worked out just fine, I found that in the days and weeks that followed, I had a great deal of trouble getting the incident out of my mind. I couldn't help but have this overwhelming feeling that I had missed something. Whatever it was, I knew it was important.

The Teacher Speaks

BUCK'S AQHA REGISTERED NAME is Alms Setter Bar with the "Bar" coming from his great grandfather, the famous thoroughbred stallion Three Bars. While he is a registered quarter horse and has a quarter-horse-type head, he is also relatively tall and rangy, with a good shoulder and the high withers characteristic of a thoroughbred. He carried the speed of a thoroughbred in his youth as well. In fact I would dare say that Buck was one of the fastest—if not the fastest—horse I've ever ridden.

When Buck came to me at seven years of age, he was what most folks would call nondescript. He was a dark, copper read (sorrel in some parts of the world, chestnut in others) with a star on his forehead and a white sock on his left hind leg. He was a bit pigeon-toed in the front, and his heels were lower than they should've been—a trait that would cause him physical problems in his later years. Other than getting a light flaxen tint to his mane and tail in the summer when the sun bleached them out, he had no outward qualities that would set him apart from a whole herd of red quarter horses.

Buck's nondescript appearance, in and of itself, made it difficult to believe that he was trying to teach me something by his unusual behavior. I mean, if he were some big, flashy, movie-star horse with tons of talent and ability and years of experience working with and for people, I could understand it. But Buck wasn't any of those things. He was just a plain horse that hadn't been ridden or even handled much before I got him.

Funny, but I guess that was one more lesson I learned from Buck—you just never know what kind of a package a teacher is going to come wrapped in.

BUCK HAD STARTED MY LESSONS by refusing my requests on two separate, seemingly unrelated occasions. During the months afterward, it began to happen more and more frequently, always in situations where we were working another horses. And the refusals all came when I felt like I really needed him to respond NOW.

When he refused my requests, I found myself having to use a whole lot more pressure on him than I wanted to. As a result, when he finally responded, it was almost always in a bigger way than I needed. That, in turn, escalated whatever situation we were in to the point where we had to go back and start all over again.

As you can imagine, his balking was very troubling to me. Not only did we have to repeat most of our work twice and sometimes three times, but in the year or so I'd been working with him before the balking started, he never once refused my requests. For the life of me, I couldn't figure out why it was happening.

Of course, when something like that happens, human nature pretty much dictates that we look at it in a negative way. I know I sure did. After all, what good could come from something like that?

It was getting to the point where each time Buck refused a request, I immediately blamed him and never looked at myself. I got upset with him for refusing and even more upset when he would finally respond too strongly, forcing us to begin again and adding hours to the jobs. At the time it didn't dawn on me that each time we went back and did a task over, I was finding a softer and better way of doing it. Nor did I realize that, each time we did things over, Buck and I were learning how to work with each other a little better. No, I was still months away from recognizing those little pearls. All I could think about was how aggravating it was that Buck was balking at the most inopportune times.

It wasn't until nearly a year after the first balking incident that I noticed something about Buck that began to shed some light on my dilemma. Oddly enough, it came not while we were riding or working together, but on a warm spring day when I happened to be watching him and the rest of the herd. I'd been replacing fence posts about a hundred yards from the water tank in the pasture. I'd emptied, cleaned, and refilled the tank just before I started working on the posts.

As was his habit, Pete, the alpha horse in the herd, went immediately over to the freshly filled tank, drank his fill, and then stood guard over it while he grazed nearby. This happened pretty much every time I cleaned and filled the big tank. For about an hour afterwards, Pete wouldn't let another horse near it. Eventually he would wander away, and the rest of the herd would come up and drink. For some reason, not letting another horse drink from the tank after it had been filled was awfully important to him.

When a member of the herd attempted to approach the tank, Pete pinned his ears and gave the horse a nasty look. Not wanting to feel the brunt of Pete's wrath, the horse quickly spun and ran away. Most of the time Pete never even had to move his feet. If the thirsty horse got too close, usually within about twenty-five feet, Pete took a couple of quick steps in its direction, sending the horse running.

By the time I finished replacing the second post, Pete had easily chased five or six horses from the tank. I'd just moved my tools over to the third rotted post when I happened to look up and see Buck making his way over to get a drink. At first I didn't give it a second thought. I figured that Pete would chase him away, just as he had all the others.

I knocked the rails off the old post, and in the process, the post snapped off at the ground. As I went about the business of digging out the rotten end, it dawned on me that several minutes had passed without the telltale sound of thundering hooves from horses running back up the hill. I wondered why I hadn't heard Buck running away, so I turned to see what was going on.

There, about thirty feet from the tank, was Buck, standing quietly, his head down and one hind foot cocked in a relaxed manner. Pete was grazing with one ear on Buck and a sort of upset look on his face. I found myself mesmerized by the two horses, and as much as I like planting fence posts, I couldn't seem to pull myself away from what was going on.

Every once in a while Pete raised his head and pinned his ears, but he didn't get a rise out of Buck. Other than an ear flick in Pete's direction, Buck showed little concern. That seemed to get under Pete's skin, and after four or five minutes, Pete suddenly flew into an all-out attack on Buck.

Pete galloped up the hill toward Buck, ears pinned and teeth bared. Buck held his ground until the very last second. Then, with Pete speeding toward him and less than five feet between them, Buck quickly, but calmly, stepped to his left, sending Pete speeding past him like a bull running under a matador's red cape. While Pete tried to catch his balance after his failed attack, Buck sort of jog-trotted nonchalantly over to the water tank, put his head down, and started to drink.

Pete ended up well past the place Buck had been standing and was now a good fifty feet away. He stood on the hill watching Buck drink. I guess it was too much work to go back down, or he decided the tank no longer needed guarding. Either way, Pete turned and joined the rest of the grazing herd.

Buck slowly pulled his head from the tank, stretched his neck out slightly, then opened his mouth and worked his jaw, allowing some of the water, along with pieces of unchewed grass, to fall into the tank. He stood for a few seconds, continuing to work his jaw, and then he slowly turned and looked at me.

He hadn't really paid much attention to me as I worked. But after all the excitement, it was like he suddenly noticed me. For several seconds he stood just looking at me. I swear, if he'd been human, I would have thought he was trying to tell me something.

Since that day I have to come to understand that most any time Buck stands and stares at me like that, he is, in fact, trying to say something to me. Or, to be more accurate, he *is* saying something to me. Sometimes the things he says are pretty difficult to decipher. Other times—like the time he stood in his pen and stared at me instead of eating the pellets I'd given him—they're relatively easy to figure out.

In that case it was simply a process of elimination. When I walked up to his pen, he looked into his stall. When I went into his stall and checked out his pellets and water, he came into the stall, basically telling me that I was getting "warmer." When I left the stall, he shook his head and blew through his nose, telling me I was getting "cooler." Then he looked outside at the other horses eating.

A quick look outside and I could easily see what Buck wanted. The other horses had their hay. Buck didn't have his yet. I purposely hadn't put his hay in his stall that afternoon because I wanted him to clean up his pellets first. I guess he didn't like that idea. So, I threw a couple flakes of hay on the floor of his stall, and he went to eating without further delay. Just like that, a problem between horse and handler was resolved.

Of course, that problem was simple to solve only due to years of Buck teaching me how to listen to him when he was trying to "speak." Figuring out what he was trying to say the first time, when he stood at the water tank staring at me, wasn't nearly as easy, because at that stage in our relationship I hadn't learned how to listen to him.

I'M SURE THAT WHEN I tell some folks that I feel my horse was trying to talk to me, they'll either say that I'm completely nuts or they'll simply roll their eyes and tell me I'm anthropomorphizing. That is, trying to attribute feelings, thoughts, and certain behaviors supposedly inherent only to humans to an animal, in this case a horse. They may be right . . . I don't know.

It's just that I find it difficult to believe the human species has the market cornered on feelings, thoughts, and certain behaviors, such as communication. That's particularly difficult to believe knowing humans are relative newcomers to the planet. On the other hand, I really don't believe that all animals on the planet are the same, either.

What I do believe is that most living, breathing creatures do share certain inherent traits and commonalities. At the top of the list of commonalities would be the desire to stay alive as long as possible. By staying alive we are playing our own small part in preserving our species.

Nowhere is that desire to stay alive more evident than in the flight-or-fight instinct. All animals, including humans, will run away from things that threaten their ability to stay alive. If they can't get away, they will stand and fight with everything they have in order to stay alive. That is how strong our instinct is, and be assured that, in this regard, we are no different from horses or just about any other animal on the planet.

We humans have retained that instinct even though we have worked very hard over the years at doing things that might have caused us to lose it. Things that our early ancestors would have been completely terrified of, we take for granted, such as speeding down the highway at seventy-five miles an hour inside a metal "beast" or getting into a big, shiny "bird" that takes us high in the sky. However, if we're going down the road in our metal beast and another beast jumps out in front of us, or if the big bird we're flying in suddenly drops out a thousand feet because of turbulence, our ancient instinct of wanting to stay alive comes to the surface pretty dang quick.

To take that a step further, we have also retained that instinct even though we have developed a whole slew of religions that tell us of the most glorious rewards that wait for us when we die. Even with that carrot dangling in front of us, we still do whatever it takes to stay here, just like every other animal that has graced the earth—with the possible exception of the lemming.

For me, it only stands to reason that if we share one basic instinct with other species, surely there are likely to be more things we share. For instance, generally speaking, in the world of animals (humans included), there is a sort of live-and-let-live attitude. Sure, some animals are predators and some are prey. But very few animals, including predators, kill just to kill. On some level, we all instinctively know that in order for us to survive we must make sure that other species of animals also survive. Even though there are prey and predators, both have learned how to survive and, in one manner or another, live together on a sustainable level.

I believe one of the reasons we're all able to survive together is that we have a basic understanding of one another. For instance, any animal that has been fearful will likely recognize fear in another animal, even if that animal is a different species. Any animal that has been angry will recognize anger in another animal. By the same token, I believe that any animal that has ever wanted to get along with another animal will recognize when another animal is trying to get along with it.

I might take that thought a step further and say that if another animal does not pose a threat, then the first animal might be able to act more like itself, showing its true personality, rather than acting in a defensive or aggressive manner. Basically, the animal can be who he is.

It seems to me that when that happens, a door opens for communication between animals of different species and, in some cases, even between animals that are dire enemies.

A quick look around the animal world is all one needs to understand what I'm talking about here. It is not uncommon in some parts of the world to see a little bird standing in the open mouths of an alligator as it picks the parasites from the alligator's mouth. The alligator could easily snap its jaws shut, killing the bird, but somewhere along the line it has communicated to the bird that it won't, and the bird understands it's safe.

Lions in Africa will rest in the shade of a tree having eaten a fresh kill, while prey animals graze peacefully nearby. Again, the prey animals know that they aren't in any danger, due to thousands of years of communication between the species. They know that once the lions have eaten, they won't be hunting again for a time and so they are safe, at least for a while.

I'm sure there are countless other examples of this type of communication, but the idea is the same. It's not uncommon in the animal world for different species to interact and even teach things to each other—particularly when it may benefit both species on a long-term basis.

WHICH BRINGS US back to Buck. While there may be folks who will say that believing Buck was trying to show me something by the way he was interacting with me is anthropomorphizing, I would have to disagree. I'm not equating Buck's actions with those of humans. His thoughts, emotions, and instincts are those of a horse. Instead, I'm trying to translate what happens between us into something that I, as a human, can understand and that will be beneficial to both of us. In short, if Buck is trying to "speak" to me, then I need to try to listen.

Unfortunately, it was the listening part that proved to be the most difficult for me. You see, by the time Buck and I began working together, I was feeling as though I was a pretty good horse trainer. After all, I had worked with a great number of troubled horses with good success. I had started or restarted I-don't-know-how-many colts, worked with everything from mustangs to draft horses, and had prided myself on being able to help just about any horse through the issues it was having.

If the truth were told, I'd have to admit I was feeling as though I was already listening to my horses pretty well. My attitude on the situation was, *What could a relatively green horse teach me that I don't already know?* Buck seemed to me to have forgotten that I was the teacher, not him. And as it turned out, that was the biggest flaw in my thinking.

Recognizing the Problem

I WAS TAUGHT EARLY ON to respect horses, give them their dignity, and try to listen to what they have to say. In fact, I had always sort of prided myself on having a pretty good feel for what a horse was trying to communicate during training. That's the main reason it was so hard to admit that what was going on between Buck and me was actually *my* problem, not his.

It wasn't until after I'd seen the way Buck handled the situation with Pete that it began to dawn on me that I needed to pay more attention to what he was saying. Even at that, it still took several more months before things really started to fall into place for me. About that time, two seemingly unrelated things happened that finally opened my eyes.

I was doing some day work at a guest ranch, working with their horses and starting a few of their colts for them. The head wrangler was a little woman who was extremely knowledgeable, organized, efficient, and great with the horses and with the people working under her. She and her husband lived on the ranch, and as it turned out, they'd been trying to start a family for a couple of years but hadn't had much luck.

Then one day she came in and told everyone that she was pregnant. The baby was due in the off-season when the ranch was the least busy. Everybody on the place was extremely happy for her and her husband, having known how long they'd been trying to have a baby and how much it would mean to them to become parents. Everyone was happy, that is, except the owner of the ranch.

The owner was a woman in her fifties who had recently started running the ranch after her parents, who were the long-time owners, had retired. Evidently, she didn't believe a woman with a baby would be able to carry out her duties on the ranch. So, a couple of days after the head wrangler made her announcement, the owner fired her. She gave the wrangler and her husband two days to gather up their belongings and leave the ranch.

This all happened right at the busiest time of the year for the ranch, when a lot of families were vacationing there and most of them wanted horseback rides. As you can imagine, there was suddenly a great deal of turmoil in the wrangling crew, and some animosity toward the owner. Two wranglers just up and quit, leaving a miserably overworked four-person crew out of what had been a happy and efficient seven-person crew a few days before. Just like that, the horses weren't ready for rides on time. Some rides had to be canceled due to lack of help in the barn. Guests were complaining, and some had gotten so upset that they left the ranch, demanding their money back as they headed out the door.

Pretty quick, the owner was going around blaming the head wrangler for all the problems. Her thinking was that had the head wrangler not gotten pregnant, she wouldn't have had to fire her, and none of this would have happened. Most people would recognize that as a ridiculous way of thinking. The head wrangler didn't cause those problems, the owner did.

Had the owner talked with other personnel on the ranch before firing the head wrangler, she would certainly have had more insight on how her decision might affect the business. She could have saved herself and a number of others a whole lot of grief. But she chose not to do that. It seems the owner didn't give the big picture any thought whatsoever before making her decision. If she had, she probably would have chosen a different way of handling the situation.

Coincidentally, about the same time I began working with a relatively new horse that had come to the ranch. He was a very nice little gelding that they bought to use for trail rides. The horse had been owned by an older lady from a nearby town. He'd been the lady's only horse, and she rode him nearly every day on the trails near her home. In fact, he turned out to be a great trail horse, with one exception—he was terrified of having other horses behind him on the trail.

This fault was most likely due to the fact that he had always been ridden alone. Without any other horses to travel behind him, he never learned that it wouldn't be a threat if one did. So, each time a horse walked up behind him on the trails at the ranch, he suddenly shot forward in a trot or even a lope to get away from it.

This was an obvious safety problem, but the gelding was such a great horse in every other respect, the decision was made to try to help him over the problem rather than selling him. That's when he became a project for Buck and me.

I decided to start helping him by taking him into the round pen and working him off of Buck. Basically, I planned to put him on a lead line and pony him around for a while. Then I'd gradually ease Buck around to his backside, showing the gelding that having another horse behind him wouldn't hurt him.

Everything went along pretty much as planned at first. The little gelding had no trouble being ponied. He seemed perfectly happy following Buck just about any place we wanted to take him. But when we stopped and I started working Buck around toward his back end, it was easy to see that the horse was concerned.

The good news about this horse was, up to that point, he hadn't been kicking out when another horse approached him from behind. Instead, he'd just shoot forward. As Buck and I began working around to his back end, I figured that if we got too close to his hindquarters and the pressure became too much, he would simply move away from us. We had just begun our approach when I discovered how flawed my thought process had been.

I was sitting on Buck, holding the gelding's lead rope. The gelding was standing still, and Buck and I had begun moving behind him when Buck just stopped dead in his tracks. His head was near the gelding's hindquarters, and the gelding's head was near Buck's hindquarters. The gelding didn't appear to be upset and, in fact, hadn't even moved. His eyes and body appeared relaxed, and he stood with one hind foot cocked in a resting position. Because the gelding showed no outward signs of being troubled, I couldn't figure out why Buck had suddenly stopped. I didn't give it much thought, even though, as it turned out, I should have.

Well, I really wanted to get around to the gelding's back end, so I urged Buck forward. But he refused to move. I asked again, and he refused to move. I asked a third time, and for a third time he refused. On the fourth request, which admittedly I made a pretty heavy one, Buck finally moved closer to the gelding's back end. Even then, Buck's move was very slow and deliberate. Unfortunately, even Buck's caution wasn't enough to stop what was about to happen.

You see, no sooner had Buck picked a foot up and set it back down than, without warning, the little horse flew into one of the biggest fits I'd ever seen. It took us a little while to get him settled down following the big explosion. Nobody got hurt, and we did, ultimately, help him through the problem, but I sure didn't feel very good about it.

I'll be honest here. If the ranch owner hadn't fired the head wrangler only a week or so before, I'm not sure I'd have given the situation with the gelding much thought. After all, worried horses blow up all the time. It certainly wasn't anything new or even, I thought, anything to be overly concerned about. But having seen the way the ranch owner went about firing the head wrangler and suffering through the mess that followed, I just couldn't help but draw some parallels between that situation and what seemed to be going on between Buck and me.

EVER SINCE THAT DAY up in the valley when Buck first balked, something had been troubling me that I just couldn't put my finger on. The troubled feeling got stronger each time Buck refused to do something, mostly because it always happened when we were working with other horses and because each time I demanded that he move when he didn't want to, it caused some kind of major problem that we were hours, and sometimes even days, fixing.

But it wasn't until the coincidence of the firing and working with the gelding that I started putting the pieces of the puzzle together. I'd been pretty critical of the ranch owner for not thinking through the situation before making a decision to fire the head wrangler based on what appeared to be a knee-jerk reaction. The owner had so many other options available to her that would have been far more beneficial to everyone involved had she only slowed down and taken a look at the big picture. That was easy to see, at least from where I stood.

Then came the incident with the gelding. At first blush, it was just another day at the office for me. One of the horses I was working with happened to blow up on that particular day, something that normally wouldn't have bothered me too much. Although I never enjoy watching a horse struggle, it happens from time to time, especially when you work with horses that are troubled to begin with.

But this time was different. Not only had a number of similar situations popped up over the past year between Buck, me, and some of the horses we worked with, but I was suddenly seeing some pretty obvious similarities between those situations and the way the ranch owner had caused so much turmoil. I have to admit, I didn't like that comparison one bit, and I pretty much decided right then and there that it was time to take a closer look at what was going on between Buck and me.

OVER THE NEXT FEW WEEKS I slowed way down and started giving Buck's actions a great deal of thought. I mentally revisited the past year and all the situations where he'd balked. Then I tried to find similarities in the situations, which wasn't hard to do.

The most obvious was that every time he balked we were working with other horses. Another similarity was that he usually balked when I wanted him to go a little faster than we'd been going. The third, and most disturbing, was that each and every time I'd demanded he go faster than he wanted to, some kind of wreck had immediately followed.

While it didn't take me very long to figure out *what* was happening, I was still having trouble understanding *why* it was happening. For the answer to that question, I finally decided to look to the source—Buck himself.

While all this was going on, Buck lived in a herd of anywhere between forty-five and seventy-five horses, depending on the time of year. In the summer he lived with the big herd, and in the winter, the small herd. One thing I noticed about him was that, no matter how many horses he was with, he almost never had injuries inflicted by another horse. Somehow he was staying out of fights with the other horses. At the ranch we were almost always patching up one minor scrape or another on the horses in the herd. It was a daily occurrence, particularly during the summer when the size of the herd almost doubled. But Buck was one of only a handful of horses we never seemed to have to worry about. Every morning he came in off the pasture just as clean as he went in the night before.

This, it seemed to me, was the piece of the puzzle I'd been missing. The answer somehow related to the fact that Buck was always able to find a way to go about his daily business without getting into, or causing, any trouble. Then something dawned on me. All that time I considered myself a horse trainer and assumed I was teaching Buck how to work with horses while I rode him. I'd completely forgotten the fact that Buck *was* a horse and that he already knew much more about the subject than I ever will! I was suddenly very embarrassed that I'd been so ignorant, and so presumptuous.

I guess it was about then that I remembered the day I watched Buck with Pete down by the water tank. I remembered how Buck had stood, patiently waiting for Pete to make a move before he responded. When he did, it was in a way that kept both he and Pete from getting hurt, that allowed him to use the least amount of energy, and that ensured he reached his goal.

The light began to go on. But little did I know at the time just how bright a light it would be.

Lesson One:
Non-Confrontation

BUCK HAD ALWAYS BEEN A pretty laid-back horse. Nothing seemed to bother him too much; he was a master at taking things in stride. This is a great attribute for a horse in training because it makes the training process pretty easy, both on the horse and the trainer. However, the difference between Buck and most laid-back horses is that the other horses generally just go along with any training program put in front of them. In short, they just go along for the ride (no pun intended) and don't offer any input as to how the training should take place.

Buck, on the other hand, was different in that regard. Not only was he *not* just going along for the ride, it appeared that he was making a conscious effort to show me a better way of doing things. What's interesting about this is that he wasn't trying to take over entirely, like some horses might. Rather, he was very specific in choosing what he wanted to share his input on.

For example, when it came to things that he didn't know much about, such as learning how to be saddled for the first time, balancing himself carrying the weight of a rider, or responding to a rider's cues, he paid close attention to what I was teaching him and responded as well as he could.

But when it came time to perform a task that he knew something about, such as working another horse (which he was somewhat of an expert at, by the way), he became pretty adamant about having some input. Even then, instead of pitching a fit in protest when I asked him to do something "incorrect" or somehow demanding that we do it differently, he would simply and quietly refuse. Even more interesting was that after I'd forced him to do something he knew we could have done better and after I had made a mess of the deal, he just quietly went back to work and helped me fix it. It was a very humbling testament to his lack of ego.

As I thought about all this, I realized that everything Buck had been trying to tell me had been summed up in that one incident with Pete. I also began to realize that I was learning much more from him than just how to work with horses.

When I look back on it, I see there were six major lessons I needed to learn from Buck, and all of them were demonstrated during his encounter with Pete. Those lessons were:

Lesson 1: Carry a non-confrontational attitude

Lesson 2: Plan ahead

Lesson 3: Be patient

Lesson 4: Be persistent

Lesson 5: Be consistent

Lesson 6: Fix a setback and move on

The first lesson, and perhaps the most important one, was that Buck's attitude was one of non-confrontation. He was a master at finding peaceful solutions to problems he encountered with others, whether it was with another horse, a human, or a dog, for that matter.

At the water tank, a number of horses had tried to get a drink before Buck did. In each case Pete successfully chased them off. Those horses approached the tank with only one thing in mind—getting a drink. They were so focused on the water that they didn't give Pete's presence much thought. By the time they noticed him, they'd already triggered a confrontation.

Buck, on the other hand, approached the tank much more slowly. He was deliberate, not rushed. He stopped a good thirty feet away, just outside the space Pete thought he needed to protect. Finally, he waited. He chose a comfortable spot and basically set up camp. He didn't challenge Pete by getting into his space, yet he subtly let him know what his intentions were. The rest he left up to Pete.

Several minutes passed before Pete decided to charge him, and when that happened, Buck used the least amount of effort needed to get out of his way. He didn't meet force with force, but with redirection. In the end, nobody got hurt, there were apparently no hard feelings, and he had accomplished his goal. It was a win/win situation for all involved.

Even when it came to the conflicts he and I were having about our work, he was able to find peaceful solutions to them. From the first time Buck balked up in the valley to the time he balked at the guest ranch, he never once got angry with me. Frustrated, I'm sure, but never really angry. Because he never lost his temper, he allowed me to control mine. You see, had he lost his temper and begun acting up, I'd have felt forced to respond defensively to regain control of the situation. Had that happened every time, I'm sure frustration would have begun to build in me, and it would ultimately have turned into anger.

Because of the way Buck handled himself, it never went that far, even when I basically demanded that he do something he knew would be detrimental to our situation. Everything stayed pretty level between us, so I was able to begin thinking about what was going on. Had it gone the other way, I might have ended up using that energy to worry about our conflict and may have taken the situation personally, creating a me-against-him attitude. But that never happened, thanks to Buck's non-confrontational attitude. What was going on between us was enough of an irritation for me to want to get rid of it, but not enough to make me defensive.

To be honest, I don't really think Buck acted the way he did just so I wouldn't get upset. Instead, I have come to understand that that's simply the way he is. It seems to be his nature to keep things around him as quiet as possible and to keep conflict of any kind to a minimum.

This was a big eye opener for me. From the time I was very young, I'd been taught that nearly anything could be accomplished with horses if you have their trust. Before a horse can trust people, it must first be able to see us as dependable leaders who make good, sound decisions that are in its best interest. A big part of making good decisions is being able to see and head off a conflict before it becomes a problem.

It's even more important to make sure we aren't the cause of the conflict to begin with. As much as I hate to admit it, I can look back and say that I was missing that part of the equation, particularly when it came to Buck and me. I can honestly say that I trusted Buck almost from the first day I threw a leg over him. But I doubt that he trusted me very much during that same time, and that should have been evident in the way he would suddenly balk when I asked him to do certain things.

The interesting thing is that even though he didn't really seem to trust me very much, he still gave me a chance. He went along with just about anything I asked of him, unless it was something he knew we could do better. At that point, he would simply stop what we were doing and, in a sense, tell me no.

I began to see how important that concept is for a leader to understand. You have to trust that your partner is trying to do the right thing, and you have to go along with his ideas as long as he is doing okay. When it's not going well, you have to put your foot down. But it isn't enough just to put your foot down. Instead, an effort must be made to redirect things in a positive manner, so that the job gets done well and everyone wins in the end.

Even in the rare situations where a completely peaceful solution couldn't be found, Buck used additional pressure only as a last resort, and usually in such a way that it was seldom needed again. When I refer to pressure, I'm not just talking about physical force. Pressure, as people apply it, can be many things—a harsh tone of voice with an employee, a stern look at a child, a jab with a heel on a horse, a punch in the face of an attacker, or anything in between.

No matter what form or level of pressure is employed, the reason we use it is almost always the same. We are trying to make a point that hasn't gotten through any other way. For myself, using a lot of pressure is something I don't enjoy doing. I was never any good at it. Whether it was with my horses, my kids, or my employees, I realized that I would either refrain from using pressure altogether or I would, at times, go way overboard. It was hard for me to find that middle ground.

Buck never had that problem. Once I learned to listen, he was always able to get his point across without force, because he is extremely clear in his intentions. This, too, was a very important lesson for me.

UP UNTIL I REFLECTED on my situation with Buck, I'd always considered myself a pretty non-confrontational person. I wasn't very big on using pressure to accomplish things. However, after watching how Buck operated, I came to realize that I wasn't as non-confrontational as I liked to think. I also learned that using pressure perhaps wasn't such a bad thing after all, provided it was used in the proper amount at the proper time. But more about that later.

Lesson Two:
Planning Ahead

———————————

YOU HEAR THE PHRASE all the time. Everywhere you turn, someone is suggesting that you "plan ahead." *Plan ahead* for your child's college education. *Plan ahead* for retirement. Be sure to *plan ahead* for dinner and you even need to *plan ahead* so that you don't get stuck in traffic on your way to work.

I never gave this common phrase much thought before I began working with Buck. Planning ahead just seems to be part of life, something we all do every day. For most of us it's as common as eating a meal or visiting with friends. But since I started working with Buck, the phrase has bounced around in my old noggin, and I've come to the conclusion that most of the time when we say we're *planning ahead*, in reality we're only *thinking ahead*. It took some time for me to figure out there's a big difference between the two.

BEFORE BUCK DECIDED TO get a drink from the tank Pete was guarding, six horses had tried and failed. Maybe they were *thinking ahead* as they made their way to the tank, because they knew they wanted a drink and they knew how to get to the tank without running into trees, rocks, or other horses. They even picked the easiest way down the hill. But although they were thinking ahead, they were still pretty much in the here-and-now. Working in the present is natural for most horses, but it means they sometimes don't look at the big picture until it's too late. The big picture in this case, of course, included Pete.

Why those horses approached the tank with such enthusiasm puzzled me. For two years, every time I cleaned and refilled the water tank, Pete drank his fill and then stood guard. Every horse in the pasture had suffered Pete's wrath at one time or another. Yet they still came as if they hadn't seen him or given any thought to the consequences of their approach.

Maybe those horses allowed themselves to get pretty thirsty and weren't able to think of anything but drinking, becoming so focused they developed tunnel vision. With their thirst controlling them, their thought process was impaired. They allowed their situation to take control of them, instead of controlling the situation. In short, they hadn't *planned ahead*.

Buck's approach to the tank, on the other hand, was a whole lot different in that it was slow and thoughtful. He stopped his approach outside the area Pete had chosen to defend, and he was in absolutely no hurry to continue. He cocked a foot, lowered his head, and seemed to go to sleep. It was obvious he wanted a drink, but Buck appeared to have begun his approach before he was too thirsty to plan things out.

Pete still felt the need to run Buck off, but now he had to travel a good distance to do it. Forcing Pete to run up the slope to get to him apparently did a couple of things in Buck's favor. The first was that it gave Buck time to prepare a response. It also pulled Pete outside the boundary that he was trying to protect.

Buck's sideways step caused Pete to rush past him, putting Pete even farther outside the area he was protecting. Suddenly Pete no longer had anything to protect, so he just went back to grazing. Buck was free to move to the tank and get his drink. It seemed like pretty good planning to me.

I can hear the groans and I know you're thinking, *What's happened to ol' Mark? He used to be such a nice fellow. All those years in the sun must have caused him to go 'round the bend. Heck, everybody knows that animals aren't smart enough to know how to plan ahead! If they did, that would mean they could deduce things and even make reasonable assumptions about the future. If that were the case, it would put animals on the same playing field as us humans. And we can't have that now, can we?*

Okay, okay, hold on. Before you get too upset, let's slow down and give this some thought. Again, keep in mind that we humans are relative newcomers to the planet and, like other species, survival is our primary goal. To survive, all species need to be able to make reasonable assumptions about the future to some degree. To understand this, all we need to do is go out and watch how animals do things in the wild or, for that matter, in more domestic settings.

A great way to understand this is to look at a band of wild horses and how they go about getting to a watering hole. A herd will travel great distances away from water while grazing. Yet, they time their journey back to water so that no horse in the herd dies of thirst. Few horses can go without water for more than about three days, so how the herd times their journey suddenly becomes a pretty amazing feat. They obviously have to start their trek to water before they get thirsty. An already dehydrated horse that has to travel maybe a hundred miles through an arid landscape probably isn't going to make it.

Despite the need to range far from water to graze, wild horses have no trouble surviving, and even thriving. The simple fact that horses have survived in the wild for some fifty-five million years seems to be a testament to how they make certain assumptions about the future.

Now, I'm sure there are folks who will say we aren't really talking about horses planning ahead in this situation. They'd claim we're talking about instinctive behavior, something much, much different than horses actually planning. They may be right, but instinct doesn't really explain the stories we often hear about horses that have, for instance, figured out how to open the gate to their pen. And once they're out, how they go and open the gates to all the other pens on the place, letting the other horses out so they can all go play. Instinct or planning ahead?

Instinct doesn't fully explain the stories we hear about dogs that go into their owner's bedrooms in the middle of the night and wake them up because the dog smelled a natural gas leak, or smoke from a fire, or sensed a tornado coming. Seems like the instinct for most animals in that situation would be to try to save themselves, not others. Do they wake their owners because they know they need to get to safety but can't open the doors? Seems to me, in any case, that they are most certainly making assumptions about the future, which means that, in some way, they are *planning ahead*. If that's the case, it kind of shoots the theory that humans are the only animals with intelligence high enough to be able to reason.

As I MENTIONED, all the horses going to the water tank, except Buck, missed the big picture, and that's the difference between *thinking ahead* and *planning ahead*. Thinking ahead usually focuses on only one point of view, and when action is taken it often adds problems instead of solving them. *Planning ahead* involves taking the big picture into consideration, including what is currently happening and what may occur in the future. It encompasses some form of action that works in a positive way to help resolve issues without adding to them. This is what I believe Buck was trying to teach me.

To understand my lack of ability to see the big picture, all we have to do is look back at the day Buck and I were up in the valley gathering horses. After finding the herd and moving them down, Buck and I ended up between them and the draw we needed them to descend. This was the first of several tunnel-vision actions on my part that were indicative of *thinking ahead* but not *planning ahead*.

Looking back, it would have been very easy for me to take an old game trail I knew about, which would have put us in a better position. We would have ended up—undetected—well to the north of the herd, and it would have been nothing at all to move the herd into the draw and down to the catch pen. Because I was so focused on the herd itself, I hadn't even considered the game trail.

I compounded this lack of planning when we had to move around the herd to turn them south toward the draw. The three horses that seemed to be trying to follow us to the north kicked in my tunnel vision again. I was so focused on the three horses that were moving, I failed to notice the twenty-seven horses that weren't! Because I was locked on those three, I began *thinking ahead* toward the worst possible scenario—the three of them running and breaking the herd loose, sending all the horses to the open gate to the north. (Had I *really* planned ahead, I would have closed the gate *before* I went to gather the herd in the first place!)

Even after the three horses had stopped and gone back to grazing, all I could think of was getting to the north of them as quickly as possible to stop something that hadn't even happened yet! Had I just slowed myself down for a second and taken the big picture into consideration, I would have figured out that the herd most likely wasn't going anywhere anyway, and so there was really no hurry for me to get around them. That was what Buck was trying to tell me when he balked.

Even if the herd had broke and gotten through the open gate, what difference would it have made? I was there that day to gather horses wherever I found them and to follow them wherever they went, until they were eventually in the catch pens. That was my job for the day and I had all day to do it. But somewhere along the line I put a time limit on myself and was pushing myself to get it done *now*. Unfortunately, my tunnel vision, as well as my impatience, had already done me in.

Even after I spilled the herd, my tunnel vision still had a good grip on me. My only thought was of the one thing I didn't like about the situation—that we had lost the herd. While I was feeling sorry for myself, and mentally beating up my horse, Buck was switching over to his "repair" mode, but that's something we'll discuss later.

Granted, hindsight is always 20/20, making it is easy to look back on a situation and identify all the mistakes we've made. However, I have to wonder—if I'd been able to slow down a little, look objectively at the big picture, and then plan ahead *before* charging into the situation, how much easier would the day have been? Unfortunately, it seems so often our apparent need to get things done *right away* doesn't allow us to take the time we need to get things right the first time. It's funny how we almost always seem to have the time to do it over, though.

Lesson Three:
Patience

I GUESS I CONSIDER MYSELF TO BE a fairly patient person. Sure, I have my days, just like everyone else, when my patience wears thin with a situation or a person and I say or do things I'm not overly proud of. But overall, I feel patience is often my strong point.

I must confess, however, that it wasn't always that way. When I was younger and knew it all, I was always in a hurry. I felt this overwhelming need to get things done in a hurry. As a result, whenever something prevented me from completing a task quickly, I got very frustrated, and pretty soon my temper would show up. When I lost my temper, I wasn't violent, but I didn't really like myself very much. I often wished I could change, but I just didn't know how.

When I was about twenty-two years old, something happened that helped me find the change I was seeking. I went with a couple of friends on a trip through Colorado. One of our stops was the Four Corners Monument, the only place in the country where the corners of four states—New Mexico, Arizona, Utah, and Colorado—meet.

I've always like geographical oddities, and it was a very interesting place. On the spot where the states meet, set in a concrete slab, is a big brass plaque with the names of the four states. In the middle of the plaque you can stand, lie down, sit, or whatever, and have a picture taken to show that you were in four states at the same time.

About fifty yards from the plaque, there were a number of little makeshift shelters, all in a row. Each one was three-sided with a slanted plywood roof. The open side faced the monument, and each shelter had a table with some of the finest handmade jewelry and pottery I'd ever seen for sale. At each table sat the Navajo man or woman who made the items. It was at one of these tables that I learned a valuable lesson in patience.

The Navajo men and women at the tables I visited were quietly polite, often smiling kindly as they answered my questions about the stones they used in the jewelry or the price of a piece. But I also noticed that the answers they gave me were never hurried or pushed, as they might be from a salesperson in a department store. At first, this "way" took me a little by surprise. Being used to salespeople who talk fast in order to make the sale, just so they can get to the next person and make that sale as well, the Navajo's apparent lack of urgency seemed odd to me.

Looking back on it, I remember that as I left the first table, I thought this lack of urgency was laziness on the part of the man behind the table. After all, he didn't seem too enthusiastic about making a sale, and his answers to my questions were so painfully slow that I wanted to help him by answering for him.

I went to the next table, and to my surprise, the woman there acted much the same way. Her answers to my questions were very slow, and there was no urgency to make a sale. The person at the next table was the same, as was the person at the table after that.

In fact, every person at every table I visited behaved the same way—slowly, methodically, and to the point, with no wasted words.

When I reached the last table, I noticed that its owner was an older gentleman who was visiting with two of his friends, both of whom were also a little up there in years. I slowly made my way along his table, admiring the delicate intricacies of his silver work and thinking about how much time it must take him to make such fine pieces of jewelry. As I looked at the jewelry, I couldn't help but overhear the conversation of the three old men. It was then that I understood what I'd been experiencing at each table. It was patience.

As the three old men exchanged pleasant conversation, each waited quietly and patiently for the other to form his thought, put that thought into words, and share it in its entirety before one of the others did the same. At no time did one man interrupt another. At no time did one finish the other's sentence, as we so often do during a conversation with a friend. Most interesting was that they always gave each other the time needed to form the thought they ultimately shared.

As I stood listening to them, I could feel my whole life slow just a little, as if something inside me downshifted. The man behind the table leisurely turned and gave me a small nod, respectfully acknowledging my presence. I respectfully, and slowly, nodded back.

He waited to see if I needed anything from him, then after several seconds passed, unhurriedly turned back to his friends to continue their conversation. I wanted to stay, almost wishing that another half-hour of listening to them would fix the things I wanted to fix about myself. But I knew deep down that wasn't going to happen. I quietly turned and made my way back to the monument, where my friends were standing. I caught up with them in mid-conversation about where we were going next.

"Why don't we go to . . . ?" one of them started to ask.

"Back over to Mesa Verde to see . . . ," a second interrupted.

"What about Monument Valley?" another asked.

"I was going to say Arches . . .," someone started to say.

"Too far . . ."

"Not really any farther than . . ."

"Anybody hungry?"

I believe it was then that I realized just how far ahead of ourselves we really are. We're all so worried about what we're going to do next that we don't give ourselves time to enjoy what we're doing right here and now. As we headed for our van, I remember thinking to myself what a shame it was that we were missing so much of our trip, and even our lives, simply because we were in such a hurry all the time.

Heck, we were even missing some of the best parts of each other, because we didn't allow each other to form a complete thought or finish a sentence. After all, how much can we really learn about someone when we don't even let them speak in complete sentences?

From that day forward, I started to make a conscious effort to slow myself down in everything I did. As soon as I began slowing down, I noticed just how often I was interrupting people. I also started noticing how often I was being interrupted when I talked. It began to bother me that we were being so rude to each other without even realizing it. I started trying harder to catch myself when I felt the need to interrupt. When someone interrupted me, I tried to wait for them to say everything they needed to say before I spoke again. I tried to make changes in other parts of my life as well, such as slowing down when I drove and putting shopping carts in the rack after taking groceries to my car.

As time went on, I started to feel that I was getting better at the small things, like allowing people to finish their sentences, driving the speed limit, and taking more time when working with a horse. But something was still missing. Then Buck came along.

If you look up the word "patience" in the dictionary, you'll see a picture of Buck right next to it. Not really, but of all the people I know or animals I've come in contact with, I don't think I've ever met one with more true patience than Buck.

There is a saying in horse training that states, "set it up and wait." It means that when teaching a horse a task or new movement, we present the task using some form of light pressure the horse might be able to understand and then wait for the horse to *try* to perform the task. Once they offer the "try," we release the pressure. It's the release of pressure that helps the horse learn the desired task or movement.

There are two key ingredients to implementing this idea successfully. The first is the ability to *set it up* properly so the horse has some idea where to look for the solution. The most important part of setting things up is to do it in a non-confrontational manner. It's very difficult for students to learn or even to think properly if they're defensive. The second key to success is to *wait* for the try the horse offers. In order to do that, we must possess some degree of patience, and in most cases, the more patience we have, the more success we will have.

This idea of "set it up and wait" doesn't apply only to horse training. It applies, in one form or another, to most everything we do, particularly when our goal depends on the cooperation of another. In those situations, just having patience may not be enough; we must set the situation up properly. Buck was a master of setting things up properly and waiting, and it was something he helped me to understand more clearly.

IF WE LOOK BACK at the water tank situation, we can see a good example of "set it up and wait" in action. Buck's goal was to get a drink from the water tank Pete was guarding, and he could have chosen to rush down the hill to the tank, as the other horses had. At the opposite end of the spectrum, he could have taken a much more passive approach and simply found a place in the woods to wait as long as it took for Pete to leave.

Buck chose an option in the middle. He took a proactive tack by approaching the tank, stopping well short of it, and patiently waiting. He presented his idea to Pete and waited to see what would happen next. It wasn't aggressive, but it wasn't passive either.

It was the "patiently waiting" part that I really struggled with. When Buck refused my requests, I saw his behavior as everything from stubbornness to laziness. Luckily for me, it was that same patience on Buck's part that allowed me the time I needed to sort things out and ultimately helped me understand him.

AS WE WORKED TOGETHER over the years, Buck presented things to me, just as he did with Pete at the water tank. Then he would patiently wait to see if I understood what he was trying to say. From start to finish, Buck remained patient with me, whether it took a few minutes or a few years to figure out what he was saying. That's a bit humbling when we consider how fast we often push our horses to understand some of the things we ask of them.

COLT STARTING PROVIDES a perfect example of what I'm talking about here. I remember when I was a kid and Walter, the old man I worked for back then, would start a colt under saddle for the first time. Time was never a factor in this process. Sometimes we took weeks, or even months, to saddle and ride a young horse for the first time. You see, Walter's main concern during the starting process wasn't how fast he could get it done, but how well the horses understood what they were going through. Because he never knowingly moved from one step to the next without making sure the horse had a clear understanding of what was going on, he was able to keep the worry for both us and the horse to a minimum.

I'm not really sure how many young horses we started in the years I spent with Walter. Hundreds, I suppose. I can't remember one colt that bucked when we put the saddle on for the first time or when a rider first got on. As anyone who has started a colt can attest, getting a horse *not* to buck the first time someone puts a saddle on its back and tightens the cinch or when someone gets on for the first time, is a pretty fair accomplishment. To be able to do it time and time again is pretty amazing. To me, that is the true testament of what can be accomplished with patience, when quality instead of quantity is the goal.

Sadly, as I went out on my own and worked with horses in the years that followed, time gradually became a factor for me. I went from taking a month or two to get a colt under saddle to three or four weeks, from three or four weeks to six or seven days, then from six or seven days to three or four days. Finally I was doing it in one day. (There are some people who claim they can start a horse under saddle in thirty minutes, with little or no real preparation at all!) Each time I shortened the length of time I took, I noticed the colts had more and more trouble with what I presented. There was resistance, worry, and bucking . . . *plenty* of bucking.

Now there are those who say that bucking the first time we put a saddle on a horse is a perfectly natural thing and nothing to be concerned about. I agree with that to a point. Bucking is a natural thing . . . if the horse doesn't understand what's being asked of it. It's a defensive reaction to a scary situation. It most certainly isn't necessary, as Walter proved time and time again.

Somewhere along the line, I guess, a number of horse trainers, myself included, found that speed had become the most important thing in starting a colt. Sure, we all claim to take as much time as it takes to help a horse through a difficult situation, but in the end, is that what we're really doing?

Well, it wasn't long before thousands of colts were being started by any number of trainers, again, myself included, in four-day horsemanship clinics all over the country and all around the world. Often these young horses were saddled and ridden on the very first day. The colts that had some kind of preparation by their owners prior to the clinic usually didn't fare too badly. The others, the ones with limited preparation, had trouble. Many of those youngsters would pitch huge fits, bucking uncontrollably, crashing into fences, and unloading riders.

During my clinics, I tried very hard never to progress from one stage of the starting process to the next unless I was fairly certain the colt was okay with what was going on. For that reason, we usually kept the colt's stress and worry to a minimum, but even at that, I feel there was often more worry than was necessary. On several occasions, I actually refused to allow the rider to get on a colt during a clinic, because I didn't feel the colt was ready. Many of those same riders went away mumbling and kicking dirt because they wanted to get on their often totally unprepared colt in the four days allotted for the clinic. Some of the colts were so unprepared when they first showed up at the clinic that they didn't even lead properly, and yet the owners *still* wanted to get on the colt's back!

Often I would ask the owners this question: "If you plan on having this horse for the rest of its life, why are you in such a hurry to get this done so quickly?"

Their answer was usually something like, "I want to be trail riding this fall, two months from now." Or, "I want to get him ready to show by this summer," or rope or team pen.

In most cases, it was clear that the owners had *thought ahead*. (I want to rope next summer, so I'll take my horse to a clinic to be started). Unfortunately, they hadn't *planned ahead*. (I want to show my horse in a year and a half, so I'll do some preliminary things now to get my horse ready to be started. Then I'll take him to a clinic in a few months to get the basics of starting completed. From there I'll evaluate where my horse is and see what training needs to be done to meet my goal.)

Because they hadn't *planned ahead* before they brought their horse to the clinic, they often didn't have the *patience* to allow their horse the time it needed to go through the learning process. The owner wanted it to be done right now! Because the horse wasn't progressing as fast as the owner would have liked, the owner would begin to rush, often setting up a *confrontational* situation with the horse, which set things back even further.

Patience is at the core of many of Buck's lessons, including planning ahead and being non-confrontational.

Now GRANTED, not everyone who brought a colt to my clinics was in such a big hurry to get things done. Several people, particularly toward the end of the time I was doing colt-starting clinics, told me that they weren't in any hurry to get their colt under saddle. And the great thing was, they meant it!

However, I finally came to the conclusion that, for me, four days was just not enough time to start a colt the way I'd like to. So, the year after I retired Buck, I simply stopped doing colt-starting clinics. I've returned to starting colts in weeks rather than days and have consciously worked on developing the kind of patience that Buck showed me.

I know it will probably take me quite a little time to achieve that goal. Maybe even more time than I ultimately have. But then, I guess that's just one more of the many legacies Buck has left me with—patience.

Lesson Four:
Persistence

_____

THE FIRST FEW TIMES Buck balked, I just thought of his behavior as negative, as I suppose most horse folks would. After all, a horse balking at a rider's request is inherently a bad thing and should not be tolerated. What other way was there to think about it?

For years, most people, myself included, were taught that if a horse doesn't do what you want, when you want, it must be refusing. Horses refuse, we were told, for one of three reasons: they don't understand your request; they're being lazy; or they're belligerent. (Over the years, I've learned that a refusal may also come when a horse is unable to respond due to a physical problem, such as a saddle that fits poorly or teeth that need attention.) No matter what the reason, the common conception has been that if you let them get away with it, the behavior will undoubtedly get worse.

So, when Buck balked, my first reaction was to do what most riders would do—increase the pressure until I got the response I wanted. Well, I got a response by upping the pressure, all right, but not necessarily the one I was looking for. Generally he gave me a response that was much bigger than I wanted or needed, causing more problems than we had to begin with.

The reason I pushed Buck through a balk was that I couldn't get past the idea that his behavior was nothing more than a training issue, a hole in his training that I must have somehow caused, seeing as how I was the one who trained him. I decided I'd better make absolutely sure the problem got fixed. I sure didn't want the balking to continue, and I certainly didn't want it to get worse. So when he'd balk, I'd push. The next time he balked, I pushed again.

A little more than a year passed before I admitted that we weren't making much headway on the issue. He was still balking and I was still pushing. It was obvious that addressing the problem head-on wasn't working. While his balking wasn't getting any worse, it certainly wasn't getting any better, either.

The thing that frustrated my efforts to figure this out was that Buck's attitude toward me and the work we were doing never changed. Generally he wasn't upset before he'd balk, he wasn't upset during, and he wasn't upset after. So, it was obvious he wasn't balking because he was mad, upset, or afraid. Yet he was doggedly persistent in his actions. Because of this, it was difficult for me to get a good read on why he was doing what he was doing.

With the perspective gained from the passage of years, it's easy to see that I was having so much trouble because I was looking at the situation completely backwards. I was spending all that time trying to fix an unwanted behavior from Buck. The idea never crossed my mind that Buck may have been trying to help me understand something that he knew much more about than I did.

THERE'S A LINE in a popular country song from a few years back that goes, "My boss is the boss's son, and that makes for a real long day." It's a great line, but unfortunately it's too true for a lot of folks who have been overlooked for job promotions that went to a much less qualified friend or relative of the boss.

When that happens, the overlooked person, the one with the most knowledge and experience, is left with two options. He can quit and find another job, or he can stay and end up taking orders from someone who doesn't have a clue what's going on. If he stays, it will probably become his responsibility to teach the new boss the ins and outs of the job, in order for things to continue to run smoothly and efficiently.

For this to work, the underling will have to maintain a *non-confrontational attitude* so as not to upset the new boss. He'll need to head off possible mistakes the new boss is likely to make, so he'll need to *plan ahead*. He'll also need to be *patient*, as the boss struggles to understand sometimes mundane procedures. And he'll have to be *persistent* in presenting the same information over and over until the new boss understands it.

For the relationship to be a successful one, the boss will need to understand that he has less knowledge about the job he's overseeing than the people who work for him. To gain knowledge and become an effective leader, he'll first have to go through a learning process involving listening, taking advice, and putting trust in the people he's been hired to oversee. This may not be an easy task for the new boss, particularly if he allows his ego to get involved.

This is the situation Buck and I found ourselves in during our early days together. He was actually the one with the knowledge, and even though I was supposedly the boss, it was Buck, the underling, that could help me understand how to do my job better. And he set out to do that by being patient and non-confrontational, by planning ahead, and by being persistent.

One of the things I learned during this time is that there is a huge difference between belligerence and persistence. Of course, I already knew the proper definitions of the words, but that's not really what I'm talking about. I'm talking about something more; I'm talking about feel. Before my work with Buck, I'm not sure I knew the difference between the "feeling" those words convey. That sounds kind of funny, but words, just like the things they portray, truly do have a different feel to them.

Think of a belligerent person. Most likely you'll start to feel a certain emotion. Mild anger may be the best way to describe it. It's not a particularly pleasant feeling. The words often conjure up a picture of someone who may work "against" us in some way. A belligerent person generally acts in a contrary manner and probably isn't particularly interested in getting along or working with others to accomplish a common goal. In fact, belligerent people generally aren't interested in goals at all.

On the other hand, think of a persistent person, and you'll get a completely different feeling. Instead of anger, you may get a softer, more positive feeling. For me, it's the feeling that you and that person are on the same side.

Persistent people are usually the ones quietly going about their business, trying to accomplish their goals without upsetting anyone in the process. Their goals may be important to them, but not so important that they achieve them at any cost. Because of this, time isn't necessarily a factor as they set about their tasks. The persistent person is somewhere between "nose to the grindstone" and "we'll get there when we get there." For that reason, we often find ourselves wishing persistent people all the best, as they make their way along whatever paths they have chosen to follow, even if we don't stop to help them.

Those first few times Buck shut down on me, I wondered if he was being belligerent, and if the truth were known, I probably treated him like he was being belligerent. I remember thinking that he was working against me and interfering with accomplishing a goal. It was a knee-jerk reaction to behavior I didn't need and didn't want.

Even though I increased the pressure on him each time he balked, I noticed that he didn't up the pressure in return. He didn't try harder to make his point or demand that I listen to him. Instead, he persistently presented the same behavior over and over at the same level. It took a while, but I began to notice that his balks actually had a particular feel.

Over time it was the "feel" that he offered each time he balked that helped me think differently. His behavior didn't feel like a demand or refusal, as it might if he were being belligerent. Rather, it seemed like a statement. Or maybe request would be a better word. Either way, I began to feel like he was trying to say something to me.

By persistently offering the same behavior, as well as the same feel, I was left with few options but to start looking at the situation differently. And that is what ultimately helped the two of us reach an understanding.

A TURNING POINT CAME one day while we were out ponying one of the colts, Smokey. Smokey was about five months old and had been causing all kinds of trouble around the place. He was (and still is to this day) one of those horses that needs to be busy all the time. He's just not happy unless he's doing something . . . *anything!* It doesn't really matter what it is. Standing around, resting in the shade is for sissies, as far as he's concerned. He'd rather be chewing on another horse's tail or trying to figure out how to open the gate, or antagonizing the dog, or chasing a rabbit, or playing in the water tank . . . you get the idea.

We weaned him when he was about four months old, mostly because his mother couldn't stand to be around him. Since then, he had been wreaking havoc on the place and the other horses. I decided that maybe he needed a day out where he could use up all that energy in a positive way, instead of driving the other horses crazy.

So, I loaded him in the trailer alongside Buck and headed for a nearby trailhead in Rocky Mountain National Park. While I saddled Buck, Smokey chewed on his lead rope. He chewed on the saddle strings on the back of my saddle. He chewed on Buck's front leg and the side of the trailer. He tried to catch a butterfly in his mouth and pick up the brush that I inadvertently left on the fender of the trailer. Once I mounted Buck and we got under way, he tried to chew on my chaps, the back cinch on my saddle, the lead rope, Buck's tail, and anything else in his vicinity.

Smokey was so busy keeping himself occupied with mindless "fun," that he wasn't paying any attention to the trail or our surroundings. That all changed, however, when we reached our first water crossing, about twenty minutes into the ride. The stream was about twenty feet wide and maybe ten inches deep. Because Smokey had been so busy with other things, he didn't see the river until we were almost in it. When he did, he froze in his tracks. Or, I should say, he *tried* to freeze in his tracks.

From the time we left the trailer, Buck had been all business. He had his head down and was walking with a purpose, pretty much ignoring Smokey's shenanigans. In fact, prior to reaching the stream, Smokey had tried to stop along the trail to look at a chipmunk or chew on a plant or something. But Buck, without any prompting from me, just kept right on walking, basically dragging Smokey along as he went.

Buck was in his prime, extremely fit from working every day, and he outweighed Smokey by about 850 pounds. What Smokey soon found when he tried to stop was that he wasn't a big enough anchor to stop ol' Buck when Buck made up his mind that Smokey needed to be coming along. Crossing the stream in a timely manner was one of those situations.

Without slowing, looking back, or worrying about Smokey in any way, Buck marched right into the stream with Smokey in tow. Smokey skidded to the edge of the stream. Then in desperation he tried to jump it, landing about five feet from the bank, right in the deepest part of the stream. While Buck continued his unwavering march, Smokey lurched and jumped his way to the other side.

Ten minutes later we came upon our first bridge crossing. Again, Smokey locked up, and again without any encouragement from me, Buck just dragged him across the bridge. I realized that, with few exceptions, I hadn't needed to cue Buck in any way. It was as if he knew exactly why we were out there and what needed to be done. It started to become clear that Buck was taking over the training of Smokey, and all I needed to do was stay out of the way and go along for the ride.

A half-hour later we came to a T in the trail. If we went to the right, we'd be back to the trailer in about fifteen minutes; if we went left, we'd be out at least another hour before we had another opportunity to return to the trailer. Buck and I had been on all those trails about a thousand times, and he knew the trail system just as well, if not better, than I did. So, when we reached the T, I left the decision up to him as to which direction we'd go. To be honest, I expected him to take the branch that would lead us back to the trailer sooner. And that would have been fine with me. After all, this was Smokey's first trail ride, and by the time we reached the T, we'd already been out about an hour, plenty of time to my way of thinking.

Much to my surprise, Buck chose the left branch of the trail. For the next forty-five minutes or so, every time we reached any sort of obstacle, Smokey would try to stop, and Buck would just keep right on going. Each time this happened, I noticed that Smokey was putting up less and less resistance. He was doing fewer things to keep his mind (and his mouth) occupied and was beginning to pay more attention to what Buck was doing ahead of him.

By the time we reached our fourth water crossing, Smokey had decided there was no reason to fight. He followed Buck into the stream like he'd been crossing water all his life. Right then and there I felt a change in the way Buck was walking. His very purposeful walk became slower and much more relaxed. Smokey, too, was much calmer. He was walking quietly with his head down and was showing no signs of being the overly busy colt we'd started with.

When we reached the next T in the trail, I again allowed Buck to choose the direction we would go. Going to the right would put us out another hour, making the trip back to the trailer an additional three hours. The branch to the left would get us back to the trailer in less than an hour. Buck picked the shorter route.

Shortly after we turned, we came to another water crossing. It was seventh of the day, and Smokey had crossed the last three without any trouble whatsoever. As we approached the crossing, Buck unexpectedly stopped. I asked him to move forward, but he refused. It was the balk that I had felt so many times before. This time, though, instead of pushing him, I turned around and looked back at Smokey. The poor little guy was exhausted. He was standing with his head down, eyes almost closed, and hind foot cocked. At this point we'd been out for nearly two and a half hours, and with the exception of a couple of short breaks, we'd been on the move the entire time.

We sat for about three minutes before I asked Buck to move, but he didn't. I looked back and Smokey was still sleeping. We sat for a couple more minutes, and I asked Buck to move. Still nothing; Smokey was sleeping. We sat about another three minutes, and this time when I asked, Buck responded by slowly moving. He gently took the slack out of Smokey's lead rope and urged Smokey quietly forward. Smokey took first one step, then another, and we were once again on our way. Twice more on the way back to the trailer, Buck stopped unexpectedly to allow his charge to rest. Urging him to move forward went unanswered until *he* was satisfied that Smokey was able to continue.

Buck's behavior over the last year or so was finally making sense. Apparently the reason he'd been so persistent about balking in certain situations was that he'd been trying to show me some things about horses that I'd been missing. The unfortunate thing was that it took something as blatantly obvious as Smokey nearly falling asleep on the trail before I realized it. If I'd just listened to Buck instead of being so wrapped up in trying to fix a problem that didn't even exist, I could have prevented all the other problems! Had it not been for Buck's quiet persistence all that time, I'm not sure I would have ever been able to figure it out.

THAT RIDE WITH BUCK AND SMOKEY showed me in microcosm that there is a delicate balance and a very fine line we need to watch for, not just when working with horses, but in pretty much everything we do. There are times when we need to go forward with determination and energy, and other times when we must stop, wait, watch, listen, and learn.

Lesson Five:
Consistency

———————

THE INCIDENT AT THE WATER TANK between Pete and Buck wasn't the first time the two had knocked heads. Pete had been trying for about three years to find a way to push Buck around. Every time I saw him try, Buck was able to find a peaceful way to protect himself, defuse the situation, and basically leave Pete standing in a cloud of his own dust, metaphorically scratching his head, wondering what had just happened.

I believe Buck was successful at keeping Pete off balance because all Buck really wanted to do was get along and keep his day as stress-free as possible. He consistently displayed the same quiet behavior with every horse (and person, for that matter) that he came in contact with. If a horse like Pete came at him in an effort to ruin his day, he would basically shrug it off, using the least amount of energy necessary to defuse the situation. It never seemed like a big deal to him, so he never made it a big deal or allowed it to turn into one.

While Buck consistently used the least amount of energy to accomplish the most, Pete used the most energy and accomplished the least! This became so frustrating for Pete that when he fell short in an attack on Buck, there were times when he would suddenly turn and attack whatever horse happened to be closest to him. I think the thing that frustrated Pete the most was that no matter how much he wanted to fight with Buck, Buck never gave him anything to fight against, so Pete's domineering actions toward Buck became pointless, even to himself.

Buck's attitude was so consistent that over those three years, Pete's attacks on him became more for show than anything else. Watching the two of them was like watching two old men playing checkers in front of the general store. Pete was the old man who always gets beat and so is constantly yelling and accusing Buck of cheating. Buck was the old man who just sits back in his chair with his arms folded across his chest, waiting until Pete has finished yelling. Then they'd set the checkers back on the board and start another game.

THE ATTITUDE AND BEHAVIOR that Buck presented to Pete was no different than it was with me. In both cases it seems Buck was trying to get a point across. But rather than taking a bull-in-the-china-shop approach and trying to make his point at any cost, he just *consistently* went quietly about his business. He presented the same idea over and over and patiently waited for it to sink in. Acting in such a way eliminated the need for confrontation and encouraged both Pete and I to rethink our positions.

In my opinion, the key to Buck's success was that he was both *persistent* and *consistent* in expressing himself. One isn't likely to work without the other. If he'd been *consistent* with his behavior, but not *persistent*—offering the same behavior only every second or third time there was an "infraction"—it would have been extremely difficult to pinpoint the problem. If one time the "infraction" was not okay and he responded by balking, but the next four times there was no reaction from him in the same situation, I'd have been hard pressed to find the trigger for his balking.

By the same token, had he been *persistent* about showing that he had a problem, but inconsistent in the behavior he used to express himself, it would also have been extremely difficult to find a solution. Different behaviors might have been mistaken for different problems. If he was relatively indifferent to the infraction one time and went absolutely berserk the next time, you'd have to think that his first reaction was for a problem much different than the second. As a result, you might never find the real reason for his behavior.

IF YOU WERE TO LIST all the qualities you look for when choosing a friend, an employee, or a spouse for that matter, the list might include such things as honesty, integrity, patience, understanding, and fairness. More likely than not, however, one attribute missing from the list would be *consistency*. In fact, *consistency* almost never enters our minds when we think about attributes we'd like people close to us to have. I believe we just take it for granted that if someone is honest, they will be *consistently* honest. If they are patient, they will be *consistently* patient. If they are fair, they will be *consistently* fair.

In fact, about the only time we give consistency any thought is when there isn't any. Lack of consistency generally causes so much turmoil that we can't avoid noticing when it's missing. Horses struggle so much with lack of consistency that any member of a herd that isn't consistent in their behavior is either avoided at all costs or simply driven from the herd. Other animals have just as much trouble, if not more, when members of the herd or the herd itself lacks consistency. Sometimes the results are devastating.

Not long ago, in Africa, a very high price was paid by a number of elephant herds due to the interference of humans with the consistency of their herd structure. The government decided that some elephant herds in the country needed to be thinned because of disappearing habitat. They chose to kill adult elephants, leaving the non-breeding youngsters to fend for themselves.

The youngsters suddenly lost the consistency of the herd structure, along with much-needed direction from adults, and their behavior became highly erratic and dangerous. By the time they grew into young adults, they simply didn't know how to act in a responsible manner and would go on rampages in areas that the herds had traditionally avoided. Ultimately, a number of these young elephants had to be destroyed because they were terrorizing villages, destroying crops, and killing people. Humans caused this situation by eliminating the consistency that nature had provided the elephants.

The truth is, humans are no different than any other animal when it comes to the need for consistency. We see and experience it everywhere we go and in just about everything we do. A fast-food chain in New York not only has the same menu as the same chain in California, but the food all tastes pretty much the same. Your favorite television show is on the same channel at the same time every week. The knob for the hot water is always on the left and the cold on the right.

Automobile manufacturers are big on consistency. They set up their cars as consistently as possible in order to make them safe and easy for the driver to operate.

Most American-made cars, even though they come from different manufacturers, have similar controls. The gas and brake pedals in one model will be in almost exactly the same place as another model. The pedals are about the same size, the same distance from the floor, and the same distance away from each other. They're designed, using ergonomics, to fit American drivers, and they're consistent from vehicle to vehicle. Even the controls for the windshield wipers and lights are all basically in the same location and function much the same way.

In contrast, some foreign car manufacturers place controls and levers in the places where folks in their home country are used to having them, not necessarily where Americans expect them to be. As a result, it's not uncommon to find a foreign car's controls for the wiper blades, for instance, where American manufacturers put the automatic transmission shift lever. Folks from the United States are generally pretty surprised the first time they try to put their new foreign car in reverse, only to find that all they've done is spray the windshield with water fluid and turn on the wipers.

The point I'm trying to make is that most animals, ourselves included, are very much creatures of habit. It is these habits that make us tick. They help us get through the day with the least amount of stress and aggravation. They help us learn and they help us teach. But before we can develop the habits that make us who we are and who we want to be, we must first recognize the importance of consistency and learn ways to develop it.

I'VE BEEN EXTREMELY LUCKY over the years. Not only have I had the experience of working with many horses, I've had the opportunity to *watch* a great number of horses, as well. And one thing I've come to realize is that you can learn just as much, if not more, by watching horses interact with one another as you can by working with or riding them.

Usually the horses I observe are in relatively large herds, anywhere from twenty to over a hundred head, all together at one time. No matter how small or how large the herd, one thing is always the same. The horses in the herd with the most inconsistent behavior—horses like Pete—are the ones causing the most turmoil. They're also the ones that other members of the herd try to avoid.

On the other hand, horses that are consistent in their behavior from one day to the next, that don't use force to accomplish goals, and that try to get along are the ones the others seem to take comfort in. These horses, like Buck, seem to have the ability to actually draw other horses to them without even trying.

When you get right down to it, that's exactly what Buck did with me, as well. Even when things weren't going all that well between us, he still found a way to draw me in. Being non-confrontational, persistent, and consistent—even though I was probably none of these things to him in return—made me *want* to find a long-term solution to the issues we were having. It was as if he were always patiently saying to me, *Come on, Mark, you can do better than this.*

And then, just as patiently, he let me try again.

Lesson Six:
Fix It and Move On

ONE OF THE THINGS I ADMIRE MOST about Buck is the way he handles adversity. Now granted, adversity usually means something different to humans than it does to a horse. And yet, having watched Buck handle a number of potentially upsetting situations, I'm not so sure that *our* adversities need to be handled any differently.

What I came to realize was, for Buck, a setback is just a setback, nothing more and nothing less. His demeanor is always just, *Let's fix it and move on*. No need to get upset, let egos get involved, or carry a grudge.

The first time I noticed this attitude was when we were gathering horses that day up in the valley. After the herd had gotten away from us, all I could think about was how much extra work we faced. I was upset with him, I was upset with myself, and I was upset with the horses that had gotten away. All the while Buck and I searched for the herd, I sat there in the saddle screwing over the situation and basically blaming him for the entire thing. Buck, on the other hand, had already gone back to work and was concentrating on the task before us.

The cause of the problem (my trying to rush him) had apparently been forgiven and forgotten. While I was stuck in the past, Buck was already looking to the future in a productive way. The reason I was able to recognize this fix-it-and-move-on attitude in Buck was because I had experienced a similar attitude firsthand, many years before.

I was about twelve or thirteen years old at the time and working for Walter, the old horseman down the road from where I lived. He approached me one day while I was cleaning the barn and asked if I wanted to go to a horse sale. Of course I jumped at the chance, and before long we were down at the county fairgrounds looking over some sixty-odd horses that were up for sale that day. It turns out that he was looking for a very specific horse, which he ultimately found and bought.

The horse was a bay gelding that we'd watched pull a cart prior to the beginning of the sale. As I remember, he paid something like $300 or $400 for the horse, which was much more than I remember him paying ever before. Usually he bought horses for $100 or less, and more times than not, it was closer to $25 or $30. At any rate, we brought the horse home and put him in a pen next to the barn.

Just after lunch the next day, Walter asked if I'd like to go for a ride with him. Thinking that he was asking me to go for a horseback ride and never passing up a chance to do that, I happily agreed. I was headed for the tack room to grab a couple of halters when he motioned for me to follow him to a nearby shed. At first I wasn't sure what he was up to. I hadn't been in the shed very often, but I knew for sure there wasn't anything in there that we could use to ride horses with. It was a dusty, dark, little afterthought of a loafing shed that started out having only three sides and a roof. At some point, a fourth side had been added, along with an oversized sliding door.

He pushed the door open, brushing cobwebs aside as he went, and walked to the back of the shed. I followed him through the dimly lit room to the back where there were two canvas tarps. One covered something large leaning against the wall, the other covered another "something" hanging on the wall. He motioned for me to grab part of the tarp on the wall, and we pulled it off, revealing what looked like a brand-new driving harness. Even though it was in such good shape it looked new, it was obvious that it wasn't. Heck, I don't think Walter ever bought anything new. Everything on the place was at least twenty years old—with the exception of me and the horses—and most things were probably closer to sixty or seventy years old. This harness, which included the headstall, driving lines, collar, wooden hames, and all the trappings, definitely fit into the latter age group.

We removed the second tarp, revealing an old, but equally well cared for, sulky, a two-wheeled driving cart. Like the harness, it too seemed to be at least sixty years old. Only the wheels and tires appeared not to be original. They were much newer and looked like heavy-duty bicycle tires.

We took both the sulky and harness from the shed and put them by the barn. Then Walter went and got the bay gelding he'd bought the day before. For the next hour or so, he patiently showed me the different pieces of the harness, how to place the harness on the horse, and how to safely back the horse between the shafts and hook up the sulky. Once we had the gelding hooked to the cart, Walter took the lines in hand, we both climbed in, and with a quiet "get-up" from Walter, we were on our way.

For the next three hours or so, we drove all over his little horse ranch. During that time, he told me the harness we were using had belonged to his father and reminisced about having to harness the family horse and hitch it to the buggy when he was a kid, so they could drive to town for supplies. He talked of how he'd picked up the sulky back in the '40s. It was next to new when he bought it, and he'd tried to keep it looking that way even though he hadn't used it in years.

He took the time to explain to me how to drive a harness horse. When he finished, he asked me if I understood, and when I said yes, he nonchalantly handed me the lines. For the last hour of our little jaunt, I was at the lines while Walter sat with one leg crossed over the other and his arm draped over the back of the seat, smoking one cigarette after another.

Finally, it was time to call it a day. We took the horse and rig back up to the barn, and he showed me how to pull the harness and put it back properly, as well as how to put the sulky back. Then, almost as an afterthought, he told me that I was welcome to use the sulky and harness anytime now that I knew how to use it. The only stipulation was that I promise to take good care of it and always put it back when I was done.

A few days later I found myself alone at the ranch with all my chores finished and nothing to do. Walter had gone off to town, and there was no telling how long it might be before he got back. About then I remembered him saying that I was welcome to use the sulky and harness.

Keep in mind, I was still pretty young and naïve in a lot of ways when it came to the nature of horses. Because of that, I just assumed that any horse that was broke to ride would automatically be broke to drive as well. So, I went out into the pasture, chose a mare I'd been riding for the past couple months, and took her up to the barn.

After brushing her, I brought out the harness and put it on the mare just like Walter had shown me. She stood perfectly still, as if she wore harness all the time. I went back, brought out the sulky, backed her between the shafts, and hitched her up. She stood, without worry, like she'd been doing it all her life.

I climbed into the sulky and asked her to move forward, which she did without hesitation. Everything was going just as it had when I was with Walter a couple days before, when we came to the little path that led down into the front pasture. The pasture was about two hundred yards wide and a quarter-mile long. The driveway leading fro the road to the barn split it down the middle. The driveway, as well as the area around the barn, sat about four feet higher than the pasture, so there was a gradual slope down to the pasture. While going down this slope, I came to the realization that not all horses broke to ride are also broke to drive.

As we started down the slope, the weight of the cart began to push the mare downhill. That odd sensation she suddenly felt started a chain of events I was completely unprepared to handle. Without warning, the mare jumped forward like she'd been shot out of a cannon and took off running for all she was worth. The jolt nearly knocked me off the back of the cart, but I regained my balance and got myself squared up by the time we'd covered half the length of the pasture. I yelled "whoa" at the top of my lungs, only to find that, in all the commotion, the mare had apparently gone deaf.

With about twenty feet to spare before we hit the barbed wire fence at the far end of the pasture, I pulled hard on the left line and got the mare turned back toward the barn. I remember very vividly the cart tires making a sort of sizzling sound as they slid hopelessly on the dry grass while we fishtailed our way around the corner. We flew back alongside the driveway. It seemed like only seconds before we were nearing the slope we had come down, causing our current dilemma. Admittedly I wasn't thinking very well at that point, but one thing I did know was that it wouldn't be such a good idea to go back up the slope toward the barn, where we would most certainly be in the wreck of the century. So, I pulled hard again on the left line just before we reached the slope and got the mare headed back toward the other end of the pasture.

The tires made that sizzling sound as we flew around the turn, and we weren't wasting any time getting back to the fence down by the road. I tried to leave a little more room for the upcoming turn, but the mare was still panicked and the tires sizzled again. We made it back up toward the barn in record time and turned back toward the road.

We made two more very fast laps before I noticed that Walter had driven through the gate and was heading up the driveway. The mare and I flew past him going the other way and a glance in his direction showed that he seemed oblivious to my little predicament, as he was looking straight ahead while he drove toward the barn.

By that time I was getting a better handle on how to make the turns at either end of the pasture. Still, one thing was beginning to trouble me quite a bit. At the end of the pasture near the road there was a telephone pole in the corner. Now it wasn't the pole that bothered me as much as the guy wire that came down from the pole at an angle and was anchored to the ground in the pasture some twenty feet from the fence. We kept getting closer to that guy wire each time we made a turn on that end.

I'd been pretty successful up to that point in keeping us clear of the wire, but this time I wasn't so lucky. As the cart fishtailed around the corner, the right tire caught the guy-wire anchor, lurching us hard and flipping the cart, the horse, and me head over heels, sending us all into a barrel roll toward the fence. I headed one way and the mare and cart another. Luckily, the mare and cart stopped before they hit the fence, but not before the cart lost one wheel, which flew gracefully over the fence and landed in the ditch. My momentum carried me into the fence, and I had several nasty scratches to add to my numerous brand-new bruises.

It took a minute for the cobwebs to clear, but when they did, I looked up to see that the mare—still attached to the cart—had somehow righted herself. With only one wheel on the cart, she ran just as fast as she could back toward the barn. I watched helplessly as what was left of the cart bounced and shook unmercifully behind her. A sick feeling went through me as I untangled myself from the fence and climbed to my feet.

I wanted to turn around and go home right then and there. I'd made a terrible mistake by doing what I'd done and, frankly, it was a mistake that was unforgivable. I just knew Walter would tell me to leave as soon as I got back to the barn anyway. And yet, something told me that I couldn't end our time together like that. So, as much as it pained me to do so, I climbed the fence, picked up the tire in the ditch, and made the long walk back to the barn. On the way I could see the scrape marks left in the ground by the wheel-less axle of the cart as the mare dragged it back to the barn. I picked up a scrap of ripped leather scrap here, a bent buckle there, a piece of one of the lines, and a spoke from one of the wheels.

As I got to the barn, Walter was standing next to the lathered mare. He'd already unhitched her from the broken and bent cart that sat in a heap nearby. The mare was still wearing what was left of the harness, which wasn't much, and she had numerous cuts and scrapes on her legs, shoulders, sides, and hips. I felt sick. Walter was looking at the mare and petting her on the neck as I approached. I walked up, stood next to Walter, and tried to tell him how sorry I was, but nothing came out. All I could do was raise the broken and bent wheel that I'd retrieved from the ditch and offer it to him as a feeble apology.

He looked at the wheel, looked at me, looked at the mare, and took out a cigarette and lit it. As smoke rolled out of his mouth and nose, he gently reached over and took the wheel from my hand.

"Well," he said, quietly looking back at the mare, "I guess now we know how not to do that."

That was it. No "What were you thinking?" or "Look what you've done" or anything else that would have made me feel worse than I already did. Just an acknowledgment of the situation and a threatless hint that it probably wouldn't be a good idea to do it again . . . all in one short, kind sentence.

In less than fifteen minutes I had wrecked the cart and harness he had owned and taken such good care of for some thirty or forty years. Instead of looking at it as if it were the end of the world, like most folks probably would, he seemed to see it as a minor setback. There was nothing to do about it but fix it and move on. And that's just what we did. Starting that day, he began to show me how to repair leather, so I could fix the harness. He showed me how to weld, so I could repair the cart. He showed me how to replace and straighten spokes, so I could fix the wheels. Then he showed me how to fix the horse.

He never mentioned the incident again. Instead, like Buck, whenever he encountered a setback, Walter simply fixed it and moved on. He didn't look back, let his ego get involved, or hold a grudge.

Years passed before I understood why it was so easy for individuals like Walter and Buck to move past a setback. Put simply, they both looked at a setback as part of life, not the end of life. A setback is generally something that can be fixed or overcome, and the longer we stress about it, make accusations, place blame, or carry a grudge over it, the longer it takes for it to be fixed or overcome.

RECENTLY, AFTER A SUMMER of severe drought conditions here in Colorado, a forest fire started some fifteen miles to the east of where my family and I live. In a few days, the fire had moved to within about three miles of our home place, and we were placed on evacuation alert. That meant we had to get ready to evacuate our home because the fire was heading our way. So, for the next twelve hours, my family and I calmly went about the business of deciding which valuables to save and packing them in case we were told to leave. We moved a number of those valuables to a safe location. We also evacuated the horses from our place, doused the area around the house with water, moved all flammable material from around the house, and listened closely to the radio for updates on the movement of the fire.

We had not received notification to evacuate by nightfall, so we went to the nightly fire-update meeting at the local high school. At the meeting, information was shared by a forest service spokesperson on the growth of the fire, what direction it was traveling, how fast it was moving, what was being done to fight the fire, and what would be done to fight the fire in the next few days. A firefighter from the front lines got up and explained that no homes had been lost to the fire, even though it had gotten within a quarter mile of a remote subdivision near where it started. There was talk of the two pilots who had died when the slurry bomber they were flying crashed, shortly after dropping their load of fire retardant in the path of the fire as it neared someone's home. The fire was stopped and the home was saved.

The spokesperson asked if anyone had questions. A few people asked for clarification on the terminology used in the evacuation notices. Some got up and praised the efforts of the firefighters, and someone asked how long the evacuation order might be in place for those already moved from their homes.

Then one man, a newcomer to the community, got up and began to speak. Apparently upset, he began by making accusations of improprieties and mishandling of the fire during its initial stages. He said he'd heard from "someone" that the fire had been *allowed* to grow to its current size. He wanted to know why the fire wasn't put out as soon as it started. He wanted to know why more firefighters hadn't been put on the scene sooner. He wanted to know why the fire had been allowed to get so close to the town.

Some of the questions may have been valid, but none of them had anything to do with the here and now. They dealt only with things that had allegedly happened or hadn't happened in the past. They were all things that nobody could do anything about! While everyone else was concerned about the present and what was going to be done in the future, this man was so stuck in the past that he couldn't move forward. Not only that, during the time he was talking and asking questions, he effectively sucked the positive energy out of the room and stopped the forward way of thinking that had been prevalent only moments before.

The contrast between his attitude and the attitude of nearly everyone else was glaring. And, to some, his attitude was very upsetting. For me it was an impressive example of the power of negative thinking. Within a matter of minutes, one man obsessed with events nobody could do anything about had effectively shut down an entire room full of people.

It reinforced the lesson I'd learned from Buck all those years ago. If there's a setback and it's something you can fix—fix it. When we got the evacuation warning, we moved our valuables and our horses. We could "fix" that setback, and we did. There was nothing we could really do to prevent the fire from taking our house—which it didn't—so why bother worrying too much about it? This is particularly true if it's an event that's already happened. A better way to handle it is to move on the best you can, make it better, and try not to let it happen again. Worrying only takes energy away from other things that need attention and, in the end, it doesn't really help anything, anyway.

Perhaps the most lasting lesson I've learned from Buck is that the things that shape our lives—the good, the bad, the ups and downs—are only big deals when we make them that way. And truly, making a big deal out of something that really doesn't deserve that much of our attention is something we all have the ability to control.

PART TWO

Day Work

Working Together

WHAT BUCK HAD DONE, pretty much from the first time I climbed on his back, was offer me an opportunity to learn. During our early years together, I came to understand that if I paid attention, worked hard, and tried to implement the lessons he offered, I just might be able to become a better horse person. It was another two or three years before I realized there was a little more to it.

At first I had a couple of major misconceptions about the lessons I was learning from Buck. The first was that each lesson was a separate entity, completely independent from the other lessons. For instance, I believed I could be *patient* and *consistent* in a situation, but not necessarily *persistent* or *non-confrontational*. In the next situation, I might *plan ahead* and be *persistent*, but not be *consistent* or *patient*.

My second misconception was that I could use the lessons in a sort of mechanical way, turning them on and off whenever I wanted and putting them away when I thought they weren't needed.

For the lessons to be successful, nothing could have been further from the truth. All the things I was learning needed to be used all the time, and when we get right down to it, that's just one more lesson Buck taught me. He wasn't turning it on and off to suit his needs. Rather, he lived that way and he approached the world around him that way all the time, no matter what and no matter with whom he was dealing, animal or human.

This was a difficult idea for me to grasp and an even more difficult idea for me to implement. Like most folks, I had inadvertently been taught that it's socially acceptable to act differently toward different people and in different situations.

For instance, if I'm going down an aisle in the grocery store and someone accidentally cuts in front of me with his cart, the chances are real good I'll stop to keep from running into him. I might even apologize for our close shave, even though it wasn't my fault. If he notices that he cut me off, he'll probably smile and apologize; in return I'll smile and accept. However, if we play that same scenario out on the highway, the reactions of both parties will likely be very different.

Now granted, the stakes are a little higher when you're driving a car seventy miles an hour down the highway, but at their heart, the two situations are the same. Yet, more times than not, we'll handle them differently. In fact, our behavior in one situation may be at the opposite end of the spectrum from our behavior in the other.

I've talked with a lot of horse people over the years, some who are professional trainers, others who are just backyard horse owners. Many of them have told me that they have all the patience in the world when they work with their horses, but when it comes to working with people, they admit to having none. It wasn't so very long ago that I was one of those people myself.

I can remember a clinic on ground manners that I did back in the late 1980s. Right after the clinic, I told a friend in frustration that I couldn't, for the life of me, understand why so many folks had such a hard time leading their horses from one place to another. My patience was wearing a little thin at that particular clinic, not with the horses, mind you, but with the horse owners.

Ironically, that happened about the time Buck and I started working together. While I was impatiently coaching people who had come to me for help, Buck, in his quiet and unassuming way, was patiently trying to help me get through the day. The difference in our teaching styles was pretty glaring. Buck, day in and day out, was consistent in his behavior toward everyone and everything he came in contact with. On the other hand, my behavior was only consistent when it suited my needs.

For me, saying I wasn't patient with people was little more than the lazy man's way of saying I didn't want to improve that area of my life. I began to see that, even though I thought I was patient with horses all the time, in reality I wasn't. Looking back on it now, it only makes sense that I wouldn't be able to be truly patient with horses if I couldn't also be patient with people. Like being cut off in the grocery store and on the highway, at the heart of the matter, they're the same.

BEFORE LONG I CAME TO REALIZE that the six lessons I learned from Buck—carry a non-confrontational attitude, plan ahead, be patient, be persistent, be consistent, and fix your setbacks and move on—weren't really separate. They are all parts of the same thing; it's an attitude or a way of going. It's maintaining this attitude that Buck is so good at; it's the reason he had so much easy success, whether with other horses or working with me. When I grasped that concept, it was clear that using only one or two of the lessons at a time simply wouldn't work, not to the extent they work when they're put together and used as one "energy," for lack of a better word.

The more I thought about it, the more I realized I'd been way off base in my original understanding of how it worked. What we're really talking about here is a sort of circle of energy made up of the six individual lessons. When used in unison, they create an overall positive way of going. When used separately, they're relatively ineffective.

I began to understand that there was no way I could effectively carry a non-confrontational attitude without first planning ahead. I couldn't plan ahead without being patient. I couldn't be patient without being persistent or be persistent without being consistent. By being consistent I would be able to fix a setback and move on, but I wouldn't be able to do that without carrying a non-confrontational attitude. So you can quickly see that each individual lesson makes up one part of the circle, and when one part is missing, the circle can't be completed.

I don't recall ever making a conscious decision to change my way of going from who I was before meeting Buck to who I've become since then. I'm not even sure when the change began to happen. What I do know is that, at some point, I stepped on the path I believe Buck had quietly been urging me to take.

Prior to this, I was a somewhat restless individual. Not restless in the sense that I needed to be on the move constantly, but mentally restless. It seemed as though my mind was always traveling in ten directions at once. It was sometimes hard for me to truly focus on issues being presented to me, whether in my personal or professional life. At times I struggled with making solid decisions about those issues; at other times I had a knee-jerk, over-the-top reaction to something that might have had a very simple solution. When dealing with friends, family, or coworkers, I sometimes found myself being much more assertive than a situation required, and I had this overwhelming need to be right, all the time.

When it came to working with horses, I was often in such a hurry to get a correct response that I'd sometimes miss when they'd offer it. Because of that, I'd end up pushing harder than was necessary or appropriate. On top of that, I sometimes found myself rushing through training sessions focused more on the end result than on considering what the horse was going through to get there.

About two years after I met Buck, all that started to change. Over time, I noticed a gradual shift in the way I was handling myself. I talked a lot less and listened a lot more.

I started to find that it wasn't all that important that people agreed with me all the time. I wasn't giving my opinion on things unless someone first asked for it, and when I did give an opinion, it had some thought behind it.

When I worked with horses, time became less and less of a factor for me. Instead of rushing through everything just to get a response that resembled what I wanted, I spent more time teaching the correct response to the cue I was applying. I was going slower and getting one correct step accomplished in the same amount of time I used to spend getting ten less-than-correct steps done.

The biggest change was an overall slowing down of just about everything I did. Oddly enough, the slower I went, the faster things seemed to get done. The less pressure I applied, the quicker the response I hoped for. The fewer words I used, the more people listened. The less I talked, the more I heard. The less I worried, the more I could focus. The more I could focus, the calmer I stayed and the easier it was to make informed, positive decisions about things.

By slowing down, I was no longer sweating the small stuff, and just as the saying goes, I began to understand that almost everything I was doing and everything that was going on around me was small stuff. I was able to start putting things in perspective, something I'd always found difficult.

I should point out here that just because I was slowing down and looking at things differently, isn't to say that I didn't feel strongly about things. It's just that it didn't necessarily mean everybody else around me had to feel strongly about them, too. The feelings were right for me, and in the end, that was really all that mattered.

These changes certainly didn't happen overnight, and I'm still working on the process to this day. In fact, the changes didn't start on a conscious level. They began as I sought better communication with Buck and slowly turned into a better way to communicate in general.

In its simplest form, all Buck was doing in those years with me was "going with the flow." I know that probably sounds trite, and it may be a little oversimplified. But that's really all there was to it.

Look at it this way. If we take a motor boat and start downstream on a river, we'll be able to travel faster than the current. We'll make good time, the boat will be easy to handle, and we'll get where we're going with the least amount of wear and tear on the boat, the motor, and even the river.

If we turn the boat upstream, our progress will be slowed considerably. It will be hard on the boat as it pushes against the current. It'll be hard on the motor as it works twice as hard to go half as far, and it will be hard on the river as the propeller kicks up mud working against the current.

It's easy to see that, all in all, going with the energy of the river is a whole lot more effective than going against it. All we need to do is get in our boat and go with the positive flow already there. This is how I began to look at the work Buck and I were doing.

I saw the work we wanted to accomplish as a sort of river; there was already a positive flow to what we were about to do. Buck was my boat, and I could go upstream, which really wasn't the direction I wanted to travel in the first place, or I could turn downstream and go with the flow of energy that was already present. When I first started working with Buck, I was trying to get my boat upstream, fighting the current all the way. It was difficult for both of us, so Buck was constantly, quietly, urging me to turn around and go with the flow. It took a while, but I finally began to catch on. Ever so slowly I turned the nose of the boat until the current took hold and gently swept us downstream.

I know what you're thinking. Sounds pretty far fetched and maybe just a little too much like Zen horseback riding. Quite frankly, I suppose I would have thought the same thing not so very long ago. But if you think about it, you'll begin to see that there is a natural flow of energy to just about everything. Each day, we either work with the flow or we work against it. Look at the flow of energy on the highway, for instance. If everyone is driving about the same speed, a flow is established. If one person suddenly slows down, the flow is immediately disrupted, as it can be if someone is driving faster than everyone else.

There is even a flow of energy in something as simple as a conversation with a friend. As soon as the conversation starts, it begins heading in a comfortable direction. If one person abruptly changes the subject, the flow is quickly stopped, and the other person may become disoriented for a moment.

If you pay close attention, you'll see that every situation we get ourselves into, no matter how simple or complex, has this flow. You can stay out of the flow and leave it heading the direction it started. You can work against the flow, interrupting it and ultimately changing its direction, often in a negative way. Or you can get in that flow, work with it, and help it along in a positive way to its natural conclusion.

At the time I met Buck, I was a master of working against the flow, mostly because I didn't realize this natural flow existed. Even if I had known about it, I don't think I was very well equipped to do anything about it. Buck, on the other hand, armed with instinct and the knowledge behind those six lessons, was a master of working with the flow. The thing that really amazed me was that not only did he work with an energy instead of against it, he also found ways to shape it in a positive way. He'd done that effectively in the herds he lived in, and he had done it pretty effectively with me, as well.

It was that next level, I would come to understand, where true communication actually takes place. However, before I could approach that level, I found there were a few other things I needed to learn first. And for me, that was when the real work began.

Buck and Mark bringing the herd through town, heading home from summer pasture, 1987

Buck pulling slack, 1988

Buck and Mark (front of column) with Scott Bottoms (rear) on search and rescue at the Boulder Field near Longs Peak in Rocky Mountain National Park, bringing two injured hikers down off the mountain, 1990 (Jim Detterline)

Smokey, one week old, 1996

Buck and Squirt in Tennessee, 2000

Buck giving a lesson, Mark looking on, 2000

Mark and Buck in Hollywood, 2000

Setting up for "Finding the Try" video intro

Filming a segment for the video

Harry Whitney on Turbo, Mark on Buck, Horsegathering 2000

Mark and Harry, Horsegathering 2001

Mark and Buck at their last clinic, 2001

Buck working his last colt, 2001

Disengaging the colt's hind-quarters

Buck asking the colt to move over

"Follow me."

Partners

Mark/Quincy,
Aaron/Buck,
Lindsey/Squirt,
Tyler/Smokey,
going for a
ride, 2002

*"Don't worry.
I'll take care of
him."*

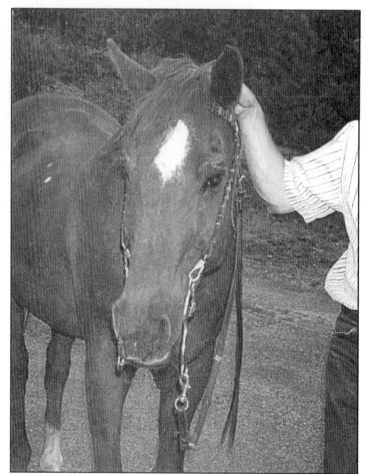

Buck, 2002

The Path

I WAS FEELING PRETTY GOOD about the direction I was going with my training. I'd been working with some pretty rough horses—horses other trainers had given up on. I was able to get the work done without rough-and-tumble training methods, and I was gaining a reputation as someone who got things done in a relatively short time when it came to "fixing" problem horses. Plus, folks seemed to like the fact that I didn't use much force to accomplish the end result.

I was getting things done, people were saying nice things about me, the horses seemed happy. Heck, life was good! Then I met Buck.

What I was about to learn from Buck, although he had to drag me, kicking and screaming, to the realization, was that success had bred complacency. And I didn't want to admit that I was, indeed, complacent. It wasn't laziness. I just wanted to improve my position in life without really improving *myself*. It happens all the time in the business world. A person improves his business skills enough to be promoted, but the *heart* of the person hasn't changed from the first day he was hired. For those people, the goal isn't necessarily to become better, but just to get higher up the ladder.

I can honestly say that I wasn't really looking to move higher up the ladder in the horse world. It just sort of happened. It seemed like one day I was guiding in the Rocky Mountains, working for this ranch or that, and the next day I was doing clinics, writing horse-training articles for *Western Horseman* magazine, and dealing with people who were coming to me for advice. It was like a wave that just picked me up and carried me forward.

As time went on, I even had this feeling that what I was doing with horses had actually turned into something special, a feeling I'd never had before. After all, when it came to working with horses, I wasn't doing anything differently than I had as a kid. Yet it was different from the things most of the other trainers were doing with horses and it was successful enough that folks saw it as more than it probably was. The problem is, once people start telling you that what you do is special, you start to believe it, if you're not careful. And that's where I was when I met Buck. I was starting to believe my own press.

I was like that fellow who's been promoted in his company. I'd improved my skills with horses, but my heart hadn't kept up. The shell of what I was doing was there, but the substance was missing. It's like kids who are promoted from one grade to the next without knowing how to read. They may appear to be moving forward, but the most important part of the foundation is left behind, so true improvement is nearly impossible. Even though I had started to believe my own press, Buck wasn't impressed.

While I was going along, perfectly content to think I was "somebody," Buck was having none of it. He knew before I did that my performance with him (and most likely with other horses as well) was pretty substandard, and his tolerance for it only went so far. He just wasn't impressed by the fact that folks thought I was doing something special.

Not long ago I attended a talk on hoof care by an experienced and highly respected master farrier, who not only has many years of practical experience working under horses, but who also has an extensive engineering background. His engineering background gives him a strong understanding of what it takes to provide structural soundness from the ground up when it comes to proper hoof care.

About halfway through his lecture, someone asked a question about the relatively new idea of the "barefoot trim" for horses. The idea behind this concept is that nearly every horse on the planet—regardless of breed, temperament, living conditions, or the job the horse is used for—should be barefoot all the time. If the horse's feet are trimmed properly and allowed to toughen up naturally, as they would if the horse were living in the wild, horseshoes would not be needed.

The instructor thoughtfully gave the idea consideration and agreed with it in theory. He noted there were a number of good things about the idea that could be very beneficial for horses under the right circumstances, but he added there were some horses that just weren't going to do well without shoes. In his opinion, between the way many domestic horses are bred, boarded, and fed, and the way they're used, keeping them barefoot would be impractical and would certainly not be in their best long-term interest.

It was hard to argue with his well-thought-out, common-sense answer. Of course, the fellow stood up and began to question the instructor further. It was evident as soon as he spoke that he was a devoted disciple of the barefoot-trim movement, and it became equally evident that he wasn't at all happy that the instructor wasn't on the barefoot bandwagon. He said that he was also a farrier and went on to share a number of his success stories about barefoot trim and how it had saved horses that had been shod but were chronically lame.

The instructor asked the man how long he'd been working as a farrier, and the man answered flatly that he had been trimming horses for only about a year. When the instructor asked what his qualifications were, the man answered that he'd begun doing the barefoot trim after attending a weekend seminar. Prior to that, he hadn't had any real experience as a farrier.

At that point, the instructor had several options on how to proceed with the man. It was obvious the man was extremely limited in his knowledge and pretty narrow-minded. It would have been easy for the instructor to engage in a verbal jousting match with the man, which the man most certainly would have lost. The instructor could have chosen to simply dismiss the man by ignoring him and moving on with his class. Instead, he allowed the man to say what he needed to say, acknowledged that his ideas had some merit, and then repeated his own point of view.

That wasn't good enough for the man, though. It quickly became apparent that he hadn't come there to learn. Rather, he came looking for an invitation to teach. Once that door was opened, he became so focused on what he wanted to say that he couldn't hear anything else that was being said, even when it was presented by someone with infinitely more knowledge and experience.

Each time the man came up for air during one of his lengthy explanations, the instructor acknowledged his ideas as valid. After some fifteen or twenty minutes of the man repeating the same thing over and over, the instructor thanked him for his thoughts and asked him to take his seat.

"But there's more that I'd like to say," the man blurted.

"There's more I'd like to say, too," the instructor countered. "And today, this is my classroom. If you'd like to hear what I have to say, then you're going to have to let me talk."

It was eloquent in its simplicity. In one brief statement, the instructor summed up the heart of the student/teacher relationship. As a student, it is our first responsibility to recognize who the teacher is. Then we must allow the teacher the opportunity to pass along information by paying attention, listening to what is being presented, and being open to new ideas.

In this situation, the instructor had effortlessly placed that responsibility directly back on the man and allowed him to decide how to proceed. He could recognize the instructor's level of expertise, be the student, and act accordingly, or he could try to be an unsolicited teacher in a class that he was under-qualified to teach.

Much to my chagrin, I recognized this was exactly what Buck had been trying to say to me when we first started working together.

As I MENTIONED EARLIER, I'd been feeling pretty good about my horsemanship skills when I first met Buck. Sure, I still had a lot to learn, but I guess I somehow thought that the information I'd need was going to come from . . . well . . . people—other trainers more experienced than me or perhaps from authors of books or magazine articles. Certainly it wouldn't come from a seven-year-old, green-broke quarter horse gelding. What I didn't understand at the time was that great teachers come in all shapes, sizes, . . . and species.

There are a number of things that separate a good teacher from a truly great one. One of the most important is how the instructor handles adversity in the classroom. When the master farrier was presented with adversity, he easily controlled what could have been a very uncomfortable situation. In the process he showed the student that he respected his views and that he expected the same in return. He left the student with his dignity intact.

When I started with Buck, I was under the mistaken impression that I was the teacher and he was the student, much like that fellow in the farrier's class. I had gone into Buck's "classroom" figuring my knowledge and experience would be enough to convince him that I knew more about being a horse than he did.

Faced with this adversity, Buck could have given up and allowed me to push him through situations that he knew could have been done better. Instead, with quiet consistence and persistence, he presented his information over and over again until I took my seat and began listening to what he had to say.

Stepping back and listening to what Buck was saying ultimately set me on a much different path than the one I'd been going down. Slowly I found my priorities shifting. People's opinion of my work had mattered to me a great deal. So much, in fact, that I wouldn't take any chances when working. I'd found a safe little box to work in where I didn't have to think very hard, and it was just fine with me. People liked my work, and as far as I was concerned, that was good enough. After all, they were paying me to work with their horses. If they were happy, I was happy. Of course, the problem with working in a box was it limited me to the point that true growth was nearly impossible.

Had it not been for Buck's insistence that I step out of my box and find a better way to communicate, I'm not sure I would have made the effort. When you get right down to it, I'm not sure I would have even known to make the effort. If anyone was ever complacent, it was me.

And yet, it wasn't just Buck's insistence that I try harder that made such an impact on me. Heck, I've had a lot of horses "insist" I do something different in one way or another over the years. It was more than that. It was his overwhelming willingness to work with me the entire time he was trying to show me a better way. It was a feeling of togetherness he offered me, even when he refused my requests, as strange as that might seem. It was his willingness to listen to what I was trying to teach him, even when I had trouble listening to him as he tried to teach me.

I know now that great teachers don't just sit around and dole out information. The great ones teach their students how to search for knowledge, while remaining a humble student themselves.

WANTING TO BECOME a great teacher/student is a wonderful aspiration. It's a path we can choose if we so desire, and it's the one Buck helped me find. The only problem, as I am discovering, is that this particular path really has no end. It does have sharp twists and turns, tall mountains and low valleys, and forks that go off here and there. Once we start down the path, the best we can hope for is to get a little farther along each day without getting too sidetracked as we go. One thing is sure, however. Remaining complacent is pretty much out of the question.

And if we're lucky, while we make our way down the path, we may meet a kindly tutor like Buck from time to time—a teacher who will stop long enough to help us keep heading in the right direction.

Positive Conflicts

LIKE A LOT OF FOLKS, I was never much good at resolving conflicts. I spent a lot of time and energy trying to avoid them, and when I couldn't avoid a conflict, I'd find myself dreading it beforehand, agonizing over it when it happened, and worrying about it afterwards.

I can see now that this was truly an ineffective way to spend my time and energy, but all I knew then was that conflict was something I didn't want to deal with. It was a bad thing, and I didn't like the way it made me feel. I looked at all conflict as negative and little more than a way to work against someone.

Even though most conflicts begin small, with both sides willing to listen to the other's point of view, often it isn't long before it escalates to the point where everybody is talking loudly, and nobody can hear what's being said. Seldom, it seemed to me, did anybody really win in a conflict. Oh, there was usually a "winner," typically the one with the loudest voice, the most money, the most aggressive personality, the biggest gun, or the largest army. But even as the loser walked away defeated, he still carried the ideals that he brought to the conflict, as well as a great deal of animosity.

As the winner walked away, he might grin at the victory, but all he did was overpower the other side. He typically hadn't changed the other person's point of view, so the victory was a hollow one at best.

This was pretty much all I'd experienced in real conflicts. Any time I'd "won" a conflict, I never felt that I'd truly won, and any time I'd "lost," I never felt like I'd really lost. Either way, all I had were bad feelings. It wasn't a healthy way to deal with conflict, but it's the way I was when Buck came along.

IT WAS PRETTY CLEAR after the first few times Buck balked that he and I were having a conflict. After all, I wanted him to do something a certain way, and he wanted me to do it differently. I was upset and confused about his seemingly contrary behavior, but as time went on, those feelings slowly began to dissipate.

The more we worked together, the more I began to see that Buck was offering me something that would be beneficial to both of us in the long run. I started to see the situation from his point of view and to understand it had merit. Of course, the big reason I was able to work through this conflict was that Buck didn't bring a confrontational attitude to it. He didn't put me on the defensive. After I figured out why Buck had balked the first few times, I no longer felt like I needed to push my point of view or force him to respond correctly. His consistent, non-confrontational approach enabled me to keep thinking through the entire situation, instead of simply reacting. I realized that the true objective of a conflict should not be to win, but to communicate.

Buck's actions during our conflict were what I would describe as being "above the fray." He evidently wasn't interested in any kind of petty argument in which both parties walk away with hard feelings. Instead, he seemed to be working hard at finding a way to turn our conflict into an exercise in real communication. I came to understand that in order for that to take place, both parties must allow the other time to think.

It sounds simple, but it was a drastic change in the way I'd thought about conflict. In my experience, nearly all conflicts had one thing in common—neither party allowed the other time to form and express complete thoughts. Most disagreements were little more than one loud interruption after another, so both parties had trouble saying what they wanted to say to get their point across. That's why, after you've been in an argument, you can always think of the absolutely perfect thing you *should* have said (but didn't)! It's nearly impossible to think of that perfect response during the heat of the moment.

I saw that most conflicts ended up doing little more than shutting down the thinking process on *both* sides. The winner of the conflict wasn't the one with the better argument. The winner was just the one whose thinking process wasn't shut down quite as soon as the other's was.

I began to understand that being in a conflict has little to do with winning or losing. What it's really about is thinking and communicating. Seen in this broader sense, conflict became less a scary thing to avoid at all costs and more an opportunity for me to work on communication at its most basic level to find an amicable solution.

I recognized that my responsibility during a conflict isn't to shut down the thinking process of the other person—it's just the opposite. If that person can keep thinking clearly through the conflict, he should be able to present his side well, enabling me to truly hear and understand his point of view. If both of us can think and hear clearly, neither of us should get defensive.

I know, I know. It sounds a little too Pollyanna, too unrealistically optimistic to work in the real world. Perhaps. But then, if you never try, you'll never know.

I'D BEEN MULLING THESE IDEAS OVER for a while without an opportunity to implement them, until one afternoon in late March several years back. It was on the last day of a long clinic tour; I'd done twelve clinics in forty-five days on three continents.

This particular clinic had gone pretty well, but even though it had been a very successful tour overall, I have to admit I was looking forward to finishing it. While I worked with the last horse and rider of the day, the familiar light haze of fatigue began to set in. It was a feeling I'd sometimes get on the last day of a clinic, particularly when I'd been on the road a long time. During that last hour, my mind began to wander, and I found myself looking forward to the next day, when I'd board a plane headed back home to Colorado. I'd finally be able to kick back and have a much-needed, three-week rest before heading back out on the road.

Near the end of the session with that last horse, I noticed a small, dark-haired woman slowly, but very deliberately, making her way from her seat near the top of the bleachers to the front row. By the time I finished the session, she was standing, stone-faced, at the arena wall.

Well, I thought to myself, *she must have seen or heard something she didn't like, and now I'm going to hear about it in no uncertain terms.*

The session with the horse and rider finished on a very good note. Over the four days of the clinic, the pair had made great progress in nearly all the things they'd attempted. They'd gone from every procedure being a major struggle, to everything being smooth and easy.

I finished the session by recapping some high points for the rider and offering him some suggestions on what he could do at home. I asked if he had any final questions for me, which he didn't, and then turned to the audience to ask if anyone had questions. Before I could even get all of the words out, the dark-haired woman, whose arms had been crossed in front of her, raised her hand.

"Yes?" I smiled.

"I've been watching your clinic for most of the day," she started rather abruptly, "and I can't help noticing that you're allowing at least half of the people in the clinic to ride with a bit in their horse's mouth."

"Yes," I replied.

"I was under the impression that you were a 'natural horsemanship' trainer," she shot back.

As soon as the words left her mouth, I knew I had a purist on my hands.

During the late 1980s and early '90s a sort of movement, if you will, erupted in the horse world. It was known as natural horsemanship. The idea behind the movement is that everything a horse owner or trainer does when working with a horse should be as natural as possible. Most folks in the movement are pretty middle-of-the-road in their beliefs. They look at things realistically and know that the word "natural" is another term for kindness and/or understanding more than it is an end result or true way to go. For the purists, however, natural means that you should ride bareback, your horse should be barefoot, and you shouldn't use a bridle. If you do use a bridle, you shouldn't use a metal bit or even place anything in the horse's mouth.

The purists often use the term "natural" as a call to arms and will fight to the death to make their point to anyone who crosses their path. Unfortunately for me, I had apparently crossed the path of one such person in the last hours of the last day of this clinic, when I was mentally and physically too tired to want to deal with her in a productive way. It was plain that she had come loaded for bear, and what was worse, she had me directly in her sights.

All I could think of, as I paused to gather my thoughts, was that I really didn't want to argue with this woman, or anyone else for that matter. I simply wasn't in the mood. What's more, her last statement about my being a natural horsemanship trainer seemed designed to get some sort of rise out of me.

On another day, in another situation, I might have come back with something defensive, such as, "Define natural." That would have undoubtedly started her down a long, winding road of explanations. Instead—probably due more to weariness than anything else—I chose to ignore her challenge and return to her original statement about the bit.

"Yes," I said, as if I hadn't heard her 'natural' comment. "Some of the riders are using bits in their horse's mouths."

"I see." She took hold of the arena rail with both hands, as if bracing for a punch. "But don't you think it's much more natural to ride a horse in a rope halter than with a metal bit?"

I paused to give the question a little thought.

"After all," she blurted, "metal is manmade and hardly something a horse would choose to put in its mouth."

I guess she had forgotten that rope is also manmade and not something a horse would naturally choose to wear around its head. But that was beside the point, and bringing it up would only make her defensive and muddy the waters.

However, one thing was clear at this point. Unless I addressed the word "natural" before long, we wouldn't be able to move forward.

"That's a good point," I said, without trying to sound patronizing. "When you refer to the world 'natural,' though, do you mean truly natural, or do you mean as natural as we can get?"

Almost without thinking, she blurted back, "As natural as we can get."

Immediately I nodded in agreement.

"Yes," I said with a smile. "That's how I look at it, too. When I work with horses, I like to try to be as natural as I can get. After all," I continued, in as light a manner as I could, "I don't think we've been truly natural since we put on loin cloths and crawled out of the cave."

There was a chuckle from the crowd, and for a brief moment, the woman's face softened into a slight smile.

"So," I continued, "I guess before I can answer your question, what we'll really need to do is figure out the definition of the phrase 'as natural as we can get'."

"Well," the woman said, this time a little slower and just a little softer, "I would say it would be whatever causes the horse the least amount of physical and mental discomfort."

"Yes," I nodded. "I would agree with that completely."

The woman was now leaning on the arena rail, instead of bracing against it.

"Have you been here for all four days of the clinic?" I asked.

"No," she replied. "Today was the only day I could make it."

"Okay," I said with a nod. "Well, maybe it'll help if I explain what we did with some of these horses over the last few days."

I began by telling her that the majority of the horses at that clinic had come in on the first day wearing rope halters instead of bits. I went on to explain that some of the horses had really struggled with them. They were unable, for whatever reason, to respond to cues through the rope halters. Because of that, the riders had to use considerably more pressure than they wanted to and certainly more than was normally necessary to accomplish the simple tasks they were requesting of their horses.

"So," I said, after going through my explanation, "in those cases, the rope halter wasn't the thing that was causing the least amount of physical and mental discomfort. In fact, the halter was causing more discomfort than simply putting the horse in a bit. So that's what we chose to do."

I turned and pointed to the horse we had just finished working.

"This horse here, for instance," I said. "When he came in on the first day, he was having trouble stopping, turning, and backing in the rope halter. Jim was using much more pressure than he wanted, just to accomplish simple things. On the second day, we switched the horse over to the bit, the problems with steering and stopping went away, and Jim is using about a tenth of the pressure."

"But doesn't the bit cause the horse pain?" she asked, with an even softer tone in her voice.

"I would say that, if used properly, no," I said and nodded toward the arena. "But maybe what we should do is ask the horse."

I turned and asked Jim to walk the horse forward, turn him to the right, then stop, which he did. The horse walked quietly forward, turned softly to the right, and stopped without hesitation or worry.

I turned back to the woman.

"I'm not saying a bit used improperly won't cause a horse pain, because it will," I said. "But by the same token, I have also seen horses whose faces were rubbed raw by people using a rope halter improperly. So I guess for me, it's not so much the tool we use, as it is the way we use it."

The woman was leaning on the rail with her chin in the palm of her hand. She nodded slightly as if agreeing.

"So," she interjected, "what you're saying is it doesn't really matter what tool someone uses, as long as it's the one that causes the least amount of mental and physical discomfort?"

"Yes," I agreed. "I guess that's what I'm saying."

"So, for one horse the most natural thing would be a rope halter," she said, "and for another, the most natural thing will be a bit."

"I would agree with that," I said, smiling.

The woman nodded, as if still mulling it over.

"Thank you," she said. "That makes sense."

She nodded, smiled, then turned and walked back to her seat.

Later that evening, I was having dinner with the clinic host. He mentioned the incident with the lady and said that when he saw her coming in the door that morning, he'd been really tempted to turn her away. He told me that she was notorious for causing problems for clinicians, asking them potentially leading questions, and then getting into lengthy arguments with them if she didn't agree with their answers.

When he saw her heading to the arena rail to ask her question that afternoon, he was sure I was in for it. According to him, she was the world's biggest advocate of using natural tack, and rope halters were at the very top of her list.

"But before I knew it," he said, pushing his empty dinner plate aside," she was smiling and agreeing with you that a rope halter may not necessarily be the most natural thing you could use on a horse. I would never have believed it if I hadn't seen it for myself, especially knowing how adamant she can be on the subject."

It began to sink in that this was the first time I could remember when I'd entered into a potential conflict without getting confrontational in any way. When it was happening, all I could think of was that I was too tired to argue. Because of that, I was more interested in trying to get along with the woman than in proving any kind of point. By doing so, she and I were able to find mutual understanding on a subject on which we apparently had opposing views only minutes before.

That situation was a real turning point for me. It brought into focus all the things I'd been thinking about. Buck had taught me to look at conflicts as opportunities to work on communication, and I'd been able to put that idea into practice. Instead of avoiding conflict, I'd made the most out of it in a positive way. It wasn't really that difficult. After all, what better time is there to work on a way to find middle ground with someone than when you're coming at a subject from different sides of the fence?

I would really like to say that since that first time I negotiated a non-confrontational conflict, it has become easier each time. Well, sometimes it has. There still are times when finding common ground is extremely difficult, if not impossible. Yet, it seems even my failures help me find better ways to deal with conflict. I've found the most important role I have is to help the other party get his side of the argument across clearly. Only when that happens can I truly understand his point of view.

In the end, conflict isn't really about winning or losing. It's about gaining knowledge and understanding, not only for another's point of view, but for our own point of view, as well.

Blending

I ONCE SAW an aerial photograph of two rivers converging. The bigger river was clear as it flowed southward. The smaller river was muddy due to an upstream storm. At the point where the two rivers met, the water from the smaller river poured into the larger one, causing part of it to become muddy.

Just below their convergence, although the rivers flowed within the same banks, they still appeared to be separate, with muddy water along one bank and clear water along the other. For a couple miles, both rivers appeared to fight to remain individuals. However, the farther downstream the water traveled, the more the two rivers began to blend. Finally, the two blended together to become one. This "new" river appeared larger and more powerful.

This natural process of blending is behind all the lessons that Buck introduced to me. When we first started working together, we were like those two separate rivers, struggling to remain separate even though we were traveling together. If the truth were told, I was struggling with the idea more than he was. Pretty much right from the get-go, he was trying to find a way to blend with me so we could work together, while I was like the little river, keeping to my own path and staying muddy. Yet, like the rivers, the longer we worked together, the easier it became to find ways to blend to accomplish common goals. We ended up much stronger because of it.

I must admit, accepting this idea of blending with my horse was extremely difficult for me at first. It is, after all, an idea that is almost foreign in our culture today. In fact (and particularly when it comes to working with horses), truly blending with another individual to reach a common goal is almost frowned upon in our society. Just look at some of the popular phrases we use in everyday conversation.

"It's a dog-eat-dog world."

"The squeaky wheel gets the grease."

"Only the strong survive."

"It's my way or the highway."

These phrases, along with countless others, offer us a snapshot of the very adversarial path we sometimes travel.

The idea of working against one another is predominant in the horse world. Most horse training is designed to find the bad a horse is doing so we can "fix" it. We don't usually look for the good, so we can build on it. The problem with thinking this way is that it automatically sets up an adversarial situation. Heck, if all we ever do is look for the bad in something, before long that's all we see.

There have been countless times during clinics when I've asked riders to tell me about their horses. They rattle off a lengthy grocery list of every bad thing the horses have ever done. But if I ask them to describe the positive attributes of their horses, they can't think of a thing to say. For those folks, blending with their horse to accomplish a task is probably the furthest thing from their minds.

I understand that way of thinking, though, because I've been in their shoes . . . more than once. The first time I realized I was seeing the bad and not the good was with Buck, and I swore I'd never let it happen again. But it did. This time, with my little horse Smokey, it really drove home the idea of blending for me.

I'VE ALREADY MENTIONED what a pest Smokey was around other horses, pretty much from the minute he hit the ground. As a baby he was always getting into trouble in the herd by sticking his nose where it didn't belong. By the time he was four months old, he'd been bitten and kicked numerous times by older horses, including his mother, who just wanted him to leave her alone. When he was six months old, he ventured to a water hole in the pasture that the herd was avoiding and ended up being attacked by a mountain lion, nearly killing him. As a yearling he'd been kicked in the mouth by a mare he was trying to terrorize and later kicked in the leg by a gelding that was tired of putting up with his shenanigans.

It seemed his mind was always working ninety miles an hour, and he had to be busy doing something all the time. He found ways to untie himself from hitch rails and open gates. If he was in a pen with cows, he'd spend the whole afternoon herding them until he could place them right in the corner where he wanted them. He once even found a way to get out of a four-strand electric fence and then opened the gates of several other pens to let more horses out. He would walk up to the fence with our border collies on the other side and hang his head over the fence just out of their reach, driving the poor dogs crazy.

I started him under saddle when he was three, and he took the entire process in stride, as if he had been ridden all his life. After maybe a dozen rides, I turned him back out. His mind, immature as it was, just wasn't in the ball game. Physically he was a little small as well, and I thought it best that he have another year or two to grow up.

I put him back to work a couple years later and found him to be just as calm and willing under saddle as before. I took him out on the road with Buck and me almost immediately, performing clinics all over the country. For the most part, he did very well in his job as a clinic horse. But there were a few things that he really seemed to struggle with, in particular standing still for any length of time.

As mentally busy as Smokey was, standing still was seldom in his program. If I asked him to stand still, he'd move his feet. If I found a way to stop his feet, he'd play with the bit. If I asked him not to play with the bit, he would paw at the ground. If I asked him not to paw the ground, he'd toss his head. In short, it was the start of an issue between him and me that I struggled with the entire year.

When Smokey first had trouble being quiet during the clinics, I wrote it off as nerves from being in a new place each week. But as time went on, I realized it wasn't nerves at all, it was just him.

The biggest problem was that I was trying to get him to *stop* being so busy all the time. I wanted the behavior to go away, and so my solution was to try to *make* it go away. I used this technique or that technique to get him to stop moving his feet or to stop chewing on the bit. And for a time, I'd be successful. Unfortunately, no sooner would I get one annoying behavior to stop than he'd do something else equally annoying.

That year Smokey and I struggled to find a middle ground, and we never really succeeded. After our last clinic of the season, I brought him home and turned him out to pasture with the rest of the horses. That gave both of us some much-needed time away from each other and a chance to think clearly about the situation.

Finally I figured out that the problem boiled down to this—every time Smokey tried to do something I hadn't asked for, I immediately tried to stop him. That left him frustrated over not accomplishing the things he started. Prior to being ridden, any time he wanted to do something, he always just went ahead and did it. He brought everything he did to some sort of conclusion, whether positive or negative. When I started riding him, all that changed.

Under saddle, not only could he no longer do anything he wanted, he was told where to go and what to do most of the time. Even when he did ask me if he could do something different during a clinic, I would basically say, *No, all I need you to do is stand still.* Well, asking a horse like Smokey to stand still meant all his unused energy showed up in other kinds of unwanted behavior.

Each time that happened, I immediately tried to put a stop to it. What I failed to understand was that by stopping his behavior I was simply putting a band-aid on the symptoms. I wasn't even coming close to curing the cause. I'd been working against him, not with him.

Now, the goal of blending is for both parties to end up like those two rivers in the photograph—it should be difficult to tell where one stops and the other starts. When I brought Smokey back to work the following year, I had a new outlook and a confident determination that I'd find a way to work with him instead of against him. The first clinic started out pretty well, although he was still a little more unsettled than I would have liked. This time when he began to move around, I simply directed his energy until he decided to stop on his own. That seemed to help somewhat, but from what I'd learned the previous year, it probably wouldn't last.

On the final day of the clinic, something happened that gave me the breakthrough I'd been looking for. One of the riders decided to put some cones in the arena and work on turns, using the cones as points to ride around. She placed the cones in an L in the middle of the arena. Smokey and I waited nearby while she quietly weaved her horse in and out of the cones before riding over to a nearby gate to work on side passing and opening the gate from her horse's back.

As the rider left the cones, I casually rode Smokey over to them so we could weave in and out of them just as she had, mostly to give him something to do. As we approached the first cone, Smokey reached down with his nose as if to touch it. I automatically redirected him away from the cone, as if to say, *That's not what we're doing.* We passed the first cone, and as we reached the second one, he once again dropped his nose toward it.

It hit me that this was the opportunity I'd been looking for. It was the perfect chance to find a way to blend with him to accomplish a common goal. Granted, Smokey's idea here was probably nothing more than to put his nose on the cone and get a good whiff of it. But I got to thinking, *As long as you're down there, let's see if we can put a task behind your idea.*

I thought we could work on getting him to tip the cone over using his nose. So, as he lowered his head to smell the cone, I gently urged him to lower his head even more by maneuvering his head with the reins. Almost immediately, I began to feel something from him that I hadn't felt before. It was a real willingness from him to work *with* me. In seconds, Smokey had dropped his head all the way to the base of the cone, and with a gentle fingertip direction from my right rein, he slowly tripped the cone over on its side.

I reached down and petted him on his neck like he'd just won the Kentucky Derby. We turned and walked away, making a small loop around the cones and giving me time to check in with the rider in the arena. I looked back at the cone lying on its side and began to wonder if, together, Smokey and I could set the cone back up. This time, instead of using his nose, I wondered if he could set it back up using one of his front feet.

We went back to the cone and maneuvered into position. Within minutes, he placed his right front foot on the base of the cone and slowly tipped it back to its upright position. I was amazed at the ease with which the two of us were able to do this. It was almost effortless, and Smokey seemed happier than I'd ever felt him before.

We left the cones and rode around for a little while longer, continuing to work with the rider on side passing and opening the gate. Several minutes passed before I decided to take Smokey back again to try "the cone thing" (as it has since come to be known). We approached another cone, and with very little urging, Smokey dropped his head and nudged the cone over on to its side. I asked him to step forward, into position, and he placed his foot on the base of the cone and tipped it upright.

I know it sounds like a pretty trivial thing, but sometimes it's the small things in life that have the most impact. This one small episode changed our entire relationship. Smokey and I had finally found some middle ground, a way to blend together to accomplish a goal. I don't know why I didn't understand it sooner. A busy mind, which Smokey had always been famous for, needs an outlet. The outlet itself doesn't really matter, as long as it's always present. In Smokey's case, just being able to use his mind and body in a constructive manner seemed to make all the difference in the world. All we had done was take his energy and use it.

From that day forward, Smokey settled down more than I'd ever seen him. Instead of moving his feet, tossing his head, chewing on the bit, and pawing at the ground, he now stood quietly and waited for direction almost all the time. If he appeared bored, we simply started working on some sort of "trick" to keep both our minds occupied. Sometimes it was something as simple as closing a gate with his nose; other times it was something a little more complicated, such as bowing on cue. In any case, we seemed to have found a way to blend together in the work we were doing, which made both of our lives a whole lot easier.

FINDING THAT COMMON GROUND, that place where two individuals meet to start working together to reach a goal, is not always easy, particularly when they have two altogether different points of view.

Not long ago I was at a large horse expo where I was giving a presentation on ground driving. On the first day of the expo, a gentleman boldly came up to me and introduced himself.

"My name is Arnie," he said, thrusting his hand into mine. "I'm into barefoot."

Of course he was talking about the natural barefoot trim for horses that has, as I've mentioned, become popular over the last few years.

"I can't help but notice that you have shoes on all your horses," he said, before I could even blink an eye. "Have you ever given any thought to the barefoot trim?"

"No," I replied. "With all the traveling I do and all the different terrain my horses need to work in, I wouldn't feel comfortable having them barefoot all the time."

Well, that wasn't the right thing to say, and for the next twenty-five minutes I was trapped in what I can only call barefoot hell. Arnie relentlessly went into every known reason (and some brand new ones) why I should keep my horses barefoot all the time. He wasn't particularly interested in anything I had to say in response and acted as if he hadn't heard me whenever I tried to say something. By the time I finally broke away from ol' Arnie, I was feeling a pretty strong dislike for him.

As I walked away, I was hoping against hope that I wouldn't run into him again. After all, I was going to be there for an entire week, and by the looks of it, so was he. If I had to deal with him on a daily basis, I wasn't sure I could be as pleasant as I had been during our first meeting.

That night I lay awake in bed feeling aggravated over my chance meeting with Arnie. I couldn't believe how rude and presumptuous he'd been. The next day I woke up in pretty good spirits, but that was shattered at breakfast when someone happened to mention that he'd also run into Arnie the day before and had received the same nonstop dissertation on barefoot trim.

I carried around a low-level aggravation for the rest of the morning, made worse by another run-in with Arnie at lunch time. Once again he went into a relentless diatribe on barefoot trim. This time, he suggested several books on the subject and expressed concern for my horses' well-being should I choose to keep having them shod. I finally got away from him and spent the rest of the day hiding out so he couldn't find me again. By the end of the day, pretty much all I could think about was how I really didn't want to see or talk to Arnie ever again.

That night, however, while again lying sleeplessly in bed, it suddenly occurred to me that I wasn't looking at the situation correctly. To say that Arnie and I had gotten off on the wrong foot would be an understatement. Within seconds of our meeting, I'd allowed him to knock me off track, but what happened after that had nothing to do with him.

I was allowing the situation to gain control of me. As I had with Smokey, I was looking at it from an adversarial perspective. I saw it as Arnie against me. And one thing was sure, it didn't have to be that way. The situation was taking way too much of my time and energy. Working against Arnie was too hard. I decided right then and there that something needed to change.

The next day I walked into the expo complex and saw Arnie sitting by himself in the bleachers. I casually worked my way over to him.

"Mornin' Arnie," I said, before he could get a word out. "How's the day treating you?"

"Good," he replied cheerfully.

"I've been giving some thought to the things you were talking about yesterday," I told him, as we met near the arena wall, "and I think I'd like to have a look at a couple of those books you recommended."

"You would?" He was surprised.

"Yeah," I said. "I have to admit, I really don't know as much about the barefoot stuff as I probably should, and it never hurts anything to get more information."

"Exactly," he said, as he rummaged through his backpack. "There's a couple of real good books you can read, particularly if you're just interested in the basics."

He pulled out a small book on the subject and gave me the contact information. I jotted it down on the back of a business card. He gave me the titles and authors of a couple more books and handed me his business card.

We talked for a few minutes about our families, the weather, the facility where the expo was being held, and some of the presenters he'd enjoyed seeing. After a few minutes, I thanked him kindly for his time and wished him luck, and he did the same. We shook hands and happily went our separate ways. Over the next three days of the expo, I ran into Arnie on a number of occasions. Each time I saw him, we greeted each other cheerfully, engaged in a little small talk, and always parted amicably.

Even after the mess that happened when we first met, we'd been able to step back and find a way to help each other reach our goals. My goal was to find a way to get along with him without compromising my beliefs. His was to pass along information on the barefoot trim program. We both accomplished our goals, and we left without any hard feelings toward one another.

In the end, maybe that's what blending is all about.

Balance

I HAD THE OPPORTUNITY a few years back to listen to an impromptu discussion between a Ph.D. and some of his students on the subject of whether or not people have a center of gravity. The Ph.D. argued that there is no such thing as a center of gravity in people. Instead, he said, what we really have is a center of balance.

He had a pretty convincing argument, but anyone who has ever fallen off a horse might disagree with him about the role of gravity in the outcome. After all, it isn't the fall that hurts, it's the impact. With perfect balance, there is no fall; without gravity, there is no impact.

Philosophy and terminology aside, I believe we have a center of gravity and we constantly use it to help improve our balance. It's that center that keeps us honest, because once we get off center, whether we're pushed or slip on a banana peel or fall off a horse, gravity inevitably pulls at us. The smaller the variance off center, the less pull, and the easier it is to regain balance. The farther off center we are, the harder gravity pulls and the more difficult things get.

Sometimes we get so far off balance that gravity easily pulls us unceremoniously to the ground. Once there, we can remain sprawled out on the ground and in everyone's way, or we can pick ourselves up and get back to center, regaining our balance.

So why am I bringing this up? I believe there are two forms of balance, the physical balance I've just been talking about, and another, very important kind of balance that we often forget about. At the risk of sounding too esoteric, this second balance is what I'd refer to as our "life balance." Physical balance is more obvious and easier to understand, but it's akin to life balance.

I define life balance as the way we deal with everyday occurrences, both good and bad. No matter which form of balance we're talking about, there is always some sort of force pushing us or some sort of "gravity" pulling at us. When we lose our physical balance, gravity is waiting to pull us down. With our life balance, the "gravity" that pulls us down can be many things—an unexpected harsh word from a friend, a death in the family, the loss of a job, a horse that won't load, or getting a flat tire on the way to work. It's anything that pushes us off track in our daily activities.

You could view life balance as the center line of a road we all travel down. When something negative happens, we're knocked off that line and we're out of balance. The worse the difficulty, the farther off the line we go. By the same token, when something positive happens, we can also be knocked off the center line in a different direction. I see our life balance as a pendulum that is always seeking true plumb.

Some folks—we all know someone like this—never get far from their center line. They seem to be able to go through life without a whole lot of stress, even when dramatic things happen around them or to them. Some animals are like this as well, and Buck is one of them. No matter how worrisome or stressful the situation, Buck never seems to get knocked too far off his center line. Buck seems able to step back from any situation, good or bad, and ask himself these three things: *What? So what? Now what?*

What? What has just happened?

So what? How does this affect me?

Now what? What do we need to do about it, if anything?

If we look at the situation up in the valley when the horses got away, we can see this attitude at work. If he could have spoken to me, I expect Buck's words to me would have been something like this:

What? Yup, the herd got away from us, all right.

So what? It's not life or death. I have a pretty good idea of where they're headed.

Now what? You can be upset with me if you want, but it isn't going to get them gathered up any faster. Go ahead and sit up there and stew if it'll make you feel better, but I'm going back to work. You can catch up when you're finished.

While the situation had little effect on Buck's attitude, it had a big effect on mine. It knocked me a good distance off my center line. It was at least half an hour before I could think straight enough to focus my energies back on the task at hand. I'd just wasted that half-hour worrying about something I could no longer do anything about! Heck, I was trying to close the barn door after the cows had already gotten out! What good was that?

There is an old Chinese parable that goes something like this:

There was an old man living in a remote village who owned a very beautiful and well-trained horse. Everyone who'd ever seen the horse wanted it for their own, and before long, word about the magnificent beast had spread to the emperor, who promptly sent a messenger to the old man's village with a request to purchase the horse for a very large sum of money.

The old man politely thanked the messenger but turned down the offer. The villagers were outraged at the old man's foolish decision, because the emperor's offer was more money than anyone had ever seen.

"Such a fool you are!" the villagers screamed. "What a bad judgment you've made!"

"My decision not to sell the horse is not good and is not bad," the old man calmly replied. "It just is."

Days later, the old man's beautiful horse ran away and disappeared into the woods. The villagers once again showed up at the old man's door.

"You foolish old man!" they shouted. "You could have sold that horse to the emperor and been a rich man. But the horse has run away and now you have neither the horse nor the money. That is very bad luck for you!"

"The horse running away is neither bad nor good," the old man quietly replied. "It just is."

A few days later, the horse returned, bringing with him thirty beautiful wild horses dancing and prancing into the old man's corral. The villagers all rushed to his house and cried, "Old man, you were right! That horse running away wasn't bad luck after all. It was very good luck because look at all the beautiful horses he has brought you!"

"These horses coming to my house is neither good nor bad," he said, tugging at his long white beard. "It just is."

Weeks passed, and the old man's only son began riding the wild horses, only to get bucked off and break his leg so badly that he would never walk properly again. Once again the villagers came to his door.

"Old man," they shouted, "what bad luck it was to have those wild horses. Your only son has broken his leg and will never again be fit to walk."

"This is not good or bad," he said, gently smiling. "It just is."

Soon, a great war broke out and all the young men from the village were called into service, with the exception of the son of the old man, whose leg had been broken in the fall from the horse. The villagers once again came to his door.

"Old man," they cried, "you were right. Your son breaking his leg was not bad luck after all. He will still be alive after all of our sons have been killed in this terrible war. Indeed, it was very good luck."

"It is not good and it is not bad," the old man said quietly. "It just is."

FOR ME, THE OLD MAN in this story represents the epitome of being in balance with one's self. No matter what happened, he was not easily moved off his center line. The villagers, on the other hand, swung from one emotional extreme to the other, never able to grasp the sheer simplicity of events around them. For them, everything was a big deal.

As much as I hate to say it, I was a lot like those villagers when I first met Buck. I suppose I still am to some degree, but at some point, I began to make a shift toward a more centered way of going. I began to realize, as Buck already had, that life itself is always in balance. For every event that comes along with an up side, there is sure to be a down side. For every down side, there will also be an up side.

There was a period in my life that was a lot like that Chinese parable, and it illustrates what I mean about the ups and downs.

YEARS AGO, the owner of a guest ranch, whom I'd done some training for, came up one day and offered me the job of ranch foreman on his place. It came with a salary, insurance, food and meals, a company truck, and a nice home on the ranch for my family and me. The owner said he and his wife were going to retire within the next five years, and when they did, they'd turn the management of the entire ranch over to my wife, Wendy, and me.

It sounded like a great offer, and after discussing the pros and cons, we decided I should take the position. We soon moved from our horse operation near town up to the ranch some seven miles away. I gave up my clients to put all my energy into the ranch. It definitely seemed like an "up."

Everything was going great, until one night about three months later when the ranch owner called Wendy and me into his office to let us know he'd put the ranch up for sale. He said we didn't need to worry, the new owners would be foolish not to keep me on as an employee. Needless to say, we felt betrayed. We began to worry about our future on the ranch, and we agonized over what would happen if the new owners didn't want to keep me on. We no longer had a place of our own to work horses, we'd given up all of my clients—we were "down."

Within a year, the ranch sold, and the new owner, a fundamentalist Christian, decided that he did, indeed, want to keep me on as ranch foreman, so life was good again. We were on the up side.

Only a few months later, however, it became clear that the new owner didn't want me on the ranch after all and was looking for a reason to fire me. The down side was back.

Before he could fire me, the bank foreclosed on the ranch, due to his inability to make even the first interest payment. The place was taken over by a group of investors, primarily run by someone who had come along with the new owner during the original purchase. He was someone I liked and admired. This primary investor ended up buying the ranch for himself and asked me to stay on as foreman, and things were looking up.

But over the next year, the owner and I began to have differences of opinion as to my role on the ranch. He wanted me to be a sort of Christian "minister" to the guests who stayed at the ranch, and I wanted only to be the guy who worked with the horses. Before long, I was fired, a definite "down."

Within two months of being fired and moving my family off the ranch, I was out performing clinics all over the world, with the help of a very talented friend whom I'd met at the ranch. I was back to work, and things seemed to be going well.

But then I discovered another down side. Because I was on the road so much—at times as much as 220 days a year—I was separated from my family for weeks, and sometimes months, at a time.

SOMEWHERE ALONG THIS five-year stretch of roller-coaster-like twists and turns and ups and downs, my sense of balance began to change. At some point my center line miraculously became more defined and mature. The highs in my life didn't really seem so high, and the lows didn't seem so low. When this change first began, I wondered if I was becoming indifferent. But that wasn't it at all.

There are still many things in my life I feel very passionate about. I have ideas and ideals that I wouldn't want to fudge on, if push came to shove. By the same token, I no longer feel that everyone around me should think as I do or that they need to be as passionate about my ideas and ideals as I am. Like the old man in the parable, I don't categorize the things that happen in my life as "good" or "bad" anymore. They are simply things that happen.

The shift that began on the guest ranch continues to this day. I keep learning, not only during big life events, but also in the smaller ones, like the one that happened during a road trip a few years ago. I'd traveled all day long and stopped for the night at a friend's place in Flagstaff, Arizona. After I arrived, we began unloading the horses, Smokey and Buck, to put them in the pasture for the night. Smokey was in the back of the trailer, so he was the first one to get out. Because of the way the trailer was set up, the horses had to back out of it. Everything was going well when, at the last minute, with his hindquarters nearly all the way out of the trailer, Smokey suddenly decided to turn around and come out head first instead of butt first. In two seconds, he was in a huge bind in the door of the trailer. With both his head and his hindquarters sticking out of the door, he panicked and began scrambling wildly. As Smokey struggled, I watched with the same sort of attitude that Buck had shown me that day up in the valley. I could feel myself assess the situation, almost in slow motion.

What? Boy, that happened fast.

So what? He's in a tough spot, but it looks like he's going to free himself.

Now what? As long as he's still moving and working on trying to get out on his own, there's no need for me to do anything. When he gets out, I'll check him for injuries.

The calmness that came over me during Smokey's struggle was becoming familiar to me. His getting stuck wasn't good, and it wasn't bad. It just was. So there was no need to worry about it until it was over. As it turned out, within seconds he'd thrashed around enough to free himself, and he literally spilled out onto the ground at the back of the trailer. After he climbed to his feet, we looked him over and noticed a few scrapes, but other than that he was unharmed.

Having Smokey get stuck in the trailer door still might seem to have been a bad thing. In the long run, though, it wasn't. Since that night, Smokey has never again tried to turn around in a trailer to unload himself.

BUCK WAS SUCH A GOOD EXAMPLE, day-in and day-out, of the "it-just-is" way of living, that he made a tremendous impact on me. I sometimes think of the countless times I got upset about something trivial, when I used more pressure on him than I should have, or when I worried unnecessarily about some situation we were in. Looking back, I can now appreciate the way he helped me get though them.

He showed patience when I had none, he accepted the pressure I used even though it may have been unnecessarily heavy, and he stepped up and saved my bacon in more awkward situations than I care to count. He took me for who I was and for where I was in my learning process with horses, and with life in general, for that matter. He never seemed to pass judgment on me as good or bad. He seemed to look at me and, even in the worst of times, say to himself, *It just is*.

Buck kept his life in balance even when I made it difficult for him. In doing so, he most certainly helped me find my own balance.

Communication

RESEARCHERS HAVE RECENTLY FOUND that elephants send out low-frequency calls that travel for miles, even through dense forests and underbrush. It allows them to communicate with one another in a way that is impossible for the human ear to perceive. In fact, if we didn't have special equipment designed to pick up those low frequencies, and if someone hadn't gotten the idea that elephants were communicating that way, we wouldn't even know the call exists. So there you go. Just when we get to thinking that we know about as much as we can about an animal, such as the elephant, they show us that they still have more to teach us.

Horses are great teachers. The problem with the way they teach, however, is that they're a lot like those elephants sending out messages at low frequencies. Not only do we have trouble hearing them, even when we do, we often completely misunderstand the message they're trying to send!

I can't imagine how many times Buck tried to communicate something to me, but because I didn't know how to listen or didn't care to try, his messages went right past me. Luckily, as the years passed, I finally woke up and saw that the things he was trying to communicate not only had merit, but were often the key to solving some major horse-related issue. Whether I'm working with a horse or with a student in a clinic, one thing I learned from Buck is to keep searching for common ground. It's always there to find. And it is that common ground that opens the lines of communication, even in a disagreement.

When true communication is taking place, it isn't necessary to have a winner in a disagreement. It is necessary for both points of view to be understood. That understanding came slow between Buck and me, but once it was there, it was like someone had opened the floodgates. Suddenly I found myself searching for understanding in every situation where communication was essential, whether between myself and other humans or between myself and horses. Sometimes I got it right and sometimes I didn't, but I always searched.

THERE'S NOTHING MORE FRUSTRATING than trying to get a horse to go in a trailer when it has decided not to. So, there we are with a perfect opportunity to work on our communication skills, and all we can think of is, *Come on! Get in the trailer. I'm going to be late!*

Generally speaking, very shortly after a horse balks at the trailer door, the horse and owner find themselves locked in a huge adversarial battle, and often nothing in the way of positive communication takes place. Before long the person, the horse, and the trailer may be surrounded by potential good samaritans—other horse people who are more than happy to help the owner get that horse in the trailer, no matter what.

Of course there are probably hundreds of reasons why a horse balks at loading, but we generally put non-loading horses into one of four categories. They could be afraid of being *in* the trailer. (Folks might say the horse is claustrophobic.) They're afraid of the actual act of *getting in* the trailer. (Some horses don't like stepping up into trailers.) It could be they are afraid of *the approach* to the trailer. (If they've been hurried while they were walking up to the trailer door, they sometimes become anxious.) Finally, some horses have never been in a trailer.

There are also those folks who would say that horses are just plain stubborn if they refuse to go into a trailer. But the reason they're "stubborn" will probably fall into one of those four main categories.

The problem with these categories is that we automatically assume that every situation will fit neatly into one of them. When it comes to something like trailer loading, we end up being a little put out when a horse's behavior doesn't fit one of the categories.

Some time back I began to see some trailer-loading problems that made me think there might be more reasons why a horse won't load. Each case caused me to work harder at the level of communication Buck had urged me to use, and in each case, I found a relatively easy solution to a problem that had seemed daunting.

The first of these problems is a phenomenon I've experienced at some of my clinics. Other trainers have told me it has happened at their clinics, as well. A horse has come to the clinic with specific problems. It goes through the clinic with its owner, and the pair ends up making great progress. The horse seems happy and content, and the rider has a new outlook on their relationship. But when it's time to go home, the horse suddenly stops dead at the trailer door and refuses to load. In almost all those cases, the horse had never had a loading problem before.

When these horses get to the trailer, they don't seem scared or upset in any way. Their behavior doesn't fit any of the convenient categories. They aren't particularly bothered by repeated requests from their owners to load. They just stand at the trailer door in a relaxed manner and refuse to go in.

The first time I witnessed this, I was asked to assist the owner after nearly an hour and a half had passed without any progress. I walked up, took the lead rope, gently petted the horse on the head, walked him up to the trailer door, and as if by magic, the horse happily stepped right into the trailer.

Over the next eight months I saw this happen on six other occasions. Horses that had never had loading problems suddenly refused to load following a clinic where some major, positive change had occurred. But if I went up and gently asked the horse to load, it willingly hopped right in.

To be honest, I always dismissed the behavior as just an odd trailer-loading issue and didn't give the matter any more thought. Then one afternoon I was called over to load a horse that had always loaded in the past. The horse got quietly in the trailer when I asked him to, and the owner remarked, "He had such a good time here, I guess he just didn't want to go home."

She was just joking, but her words hit me like a sledgehammer. Could it really be that the horse was trying to tell us something like that? After all, if we look at the situation from the horse's perspective, that may not be such a reach. Every time this happened, the horse and owner had been at each other's throats for months, sometimes even years, prior to coming to the clinic. During the clinic, which is held somewhere other than where all the bad stuff took place, major changes have occurred in the rider, mostly due to much clearer communication with the horse. The two begin to get along for the first time, and the horse's life is suddenly much easier.

To what is the horse likely to attribute the change? Well, the most obvious change is the *place* he and his owner came to ride. Maybe he's looking at the place and saying, *If this place causes this kind of change in you, I think I'd like to stay here instead of going back to the bad place where you seem to lose your mind on a pretty regular basis.*

And why would these horses load for me, but not for the owner? During the clinic, while the owner was working with the horse, I was the one giving direction and guidance to the owner. It may be the horse, an animal whose herd mentality makes it acutely aware of leadership roles, recognized me as a leader.

Truthfully, I have no solid idea why those horses would load for me and not their owners or even why they refused to go in the trailer when they'd always loaded just fine in the past.

But the fact remains that something was definitely going on between those horses, their owners, and myself during the clinic. The horse wouldn't cease to be willing to communicate just because the clinic was over.

Another loading problem that didn't fit the usual categories happened after a clinic in Tennessee. A horse that had come from out of state in a borrowed, slightly shoddy trailer, refused to load. But this particular horse hadn't loaded very well when they put him in the trailer to come to the clinic.

After an hour of trying to load the horse, the owner asked me to have a look. While the owner stood in the trailer and I stood behind the horse, I began to encourage him to load, using various means of light pressure. The gelding didn't seem too upset and moved from side to side at the trailer door with a look on his face that pretty much told us he'd already made up his mind, and he wasn't going in.

I upped the pressure a little bit at a time, and he continued to move back and forth behind the trailer without much of an attempt to go in. I increased the pressure a little more, and he tried to turn away from the trailer. We repositioned him and tried again. After several more attempts, he finally stopped, dropped his nose to the floor at the very back of the trailer, and as if aggravated, tried to grab the floor mat in his teeth.

Using the lead rope, the owner raised the horse's head and we continued. Several minutes passed and several more refusals took place before the horse suddenly picked up his right front foot and slapped it hard on the trailer floor just inside the door.

Then he did something that got my attention and made me think that something wasn't quite right with the whole situation. After he slapped the floor, he stepped back from the trailer, and with ears pricked at attention, he turned and looked directly into my eyes, almost as if he were asking me a question.

Of course, the question I thought he was asking was, *Do you want me in there?* And in fact, I actually heard myself say, as if answering him, "Yup, in the trailer."

I continued to encourage him to think about going in, and he turned and pawed at the trailer floor again. He hit the floor several times as if he were mad at it, then stepped away, turned, and looked at me. Wanting to make sure he kept his mind on the task at hand, I asked him again to get in the trailer.

By this time he was beginning to show some anxiety. He danced sideways at the trailer door and reached down and pulled at the floor mat with his teeth. He stepped back and pawed hard at the floor, giving it five or six powerful whacks with his right foot, then two or three with his left. He stepped back, turned, and looked at me again. His body was rigid and he was blowing hard through his nose.

This time, a strange feeling came over me. I don't know if it was the look I was getting from him or something in the way he was acting or just the situation in general. But one thing I knew for sure, he was trying to tell us something and he really needed us to listen.

"Hold on," I heard myself say. "Could you take him away from the trailer for a minute?"

I walked to the back of the trailer while the owner stepped out and backed the gelding away. I reached down, took hold of the mat over the floor where the horse had been pawing, and pulled it up. Underneath, I was appalled to see the wood planks were not only wet, they were very soft and rotted to the point where I could see daylight through almost all of them. I pushed down on one board with my finger and the spot gave way, opening up a small hole and exposing the ground beneath. Speechless, I slowly turned back to look at the horse that, for the first time in nearly fifteen minutes, was standing relaxed and quiet, his head down and his breathing deep and slow.

Was he trying to communicate that the floor was rotten and he was afraid of what might happen if it gave out while they were going down the road? Well, I don't know. But one thing's for sure. He definitely communicated his reluctance to us.

If I really thought about it, I could probably come up with many stories of horses making an attempt to communicate something very specific. For example, I once had a woman tell me about a time she was riding her horse into a wooded area where they had ridden numerous times. Just before entering the woods, the horse suddenly pitched a huge, unexpected fit. The rider, thinking the horse was being bad, tried unsuccessfully to make it go into the woods. After about ten minutes of fighting, the rider gave up and took the horse home. Within minutes of getting back to the barn, a massive storm raced into the area from out of nowhere, dropping golf-ball-sized hail, causing flash floods, and uprooting trees in the woods where the pair would have been riding.

OF ALL THE TIMES I'VE WITNESSED a horse trying to communicate something specific, one stands out in my mind above all others. It happened at one of my clinics, and I think about it often.

Prior to the start of the four-day clinic, the host told me that all the horses we'd be working with were there, with the exception of one. It was a big Arab stallion that the owner had been having a lot of trouble with. In fact, the horse was apparently so bad that nobody would breed their mares to him, for fear they would end up getting a baby just like him. Vets were afraid to work on him, farriers didn't want to shoe him, and the owner had come off him a number of times. This horse would be the last horse I'd work that day, and he'd be showing up later in the afternoon.

Sure enough, about mid-afternoon a truck and trailer arrived. As they pulled to a stop, I watched the trailer rocking furiously while dust billowed from the windows. Loud banging noises, as well as earsplitting screams, reverberated inside. The owner opened the door and out jumped this sweaty, screaming ball of energy in the form of a large gray stallion. Immediately the horse was on his hind legs, pawing wildly at the air. The owner brought him back to earth with a couple of well-timed pops on the lead rope, which was attached to a chain over the bridge of the horse's nose.

With much dust, noise, and fanfare, the owner got the stallion to a holding pen. There the horse ran back and forth, rearing, bucking in place, and screaming at the top of his lungs. When his turn came a couple of hours later, the owner led the horse, kicking and screaming, around the arena and toward the round pen where we'd work together for the next four days. A number of people were sitting in collapsible chairs near the round pen, and as the horse got closer, they grabbed their chairs and moved back, like the parting of the Red Sea.

The owner led the horse into the round pen, where the horse spent lots of time pawing in the air on his hind legs, screaming, and bucking in place, while the owner directed him with well-timed pulls from the lead rope. I was sitting on the top rail of the round pen watching all this happen. After the initial shock of seeing how much energy the horse had and wondering what on earth I was going to do with him, an awareness began to creep into my consciousness—the stallion hadn't tried to hurt anybody. Sure, he was making lots of noise, raising a lot of dust, and looking pretty menacing, but he hadn't really done anything "wrong."

I asked the owner if he'd mind if I came into the pen and did a little work with the horse, and he happily turned the horse loose and left the pen. I climbed down from the safety of the top rail and made my way to the center of the pen. The stallion raced wildly around the perimeter, screaming, shaking his head, and bucking from time to time. He made about four laps before he even realized I was in the pen with him. When he finally saw me, he turned and charged in my direction.

When I entered the pen, I was betting that this horse, even with all his noise, rearing, bucking, and bravado, wasn't interested in hurting anybody. Within the next few seconds, I'd find out if I had won that bet.

As he charged, I faced a decision. I was standing there with only a halter and lead rope hanging in the crook of my arm to defend myself. If I was right about him not wanting to hurt anybody, I was going to be okay and wouldn't need them. If I defended myself when it wasn't warranted, he might see my behavior as confrontational, and I'd be just one more person who didn't want to get along with him. On the other hand, if I needed to defend myself but didn't, what happened next could ruin my day.

Staying as calm as I could, I reached for the lead rope, just in case, and waited for what seemed an eternity. The stallion covered the ground between us very quickly but stopped some six or seven feet away and reared straight up in the air. He came back down, reared up again, came back down, shook his head, looked at me for a brief second or two, then turned and ran off. He made a couple of laps and came back toward me, repeating his behavior of rearing, shaking his head, and running off.

He did this three more times before circling closely around me at a trot. He finally stopped at my right side, facing the same direction I was, and quietly dropped his head. I reached over and stroked him lightly on his shoulder. He flinched at my touch, then relaxed and let out a small sigh.

This was the beginning of four days of communication between humans and a horse that seemed to want nothing more than to be treated with a little dignity and kindness. We spent the rest of that day working on some light groundwork that he did very quietly and willingly. We made a point that day not to defend ourselves against him, and he slowly, but surely, tried not to give us a reason to.

The second day we worked on longeing and ground driving, which he had very little trouble with, and we began to find out just how responsive and willing he really was. The softness that he offered every step of the way amazed us. We began to see that he was very sensitive; the amount of pressure used on him in the past must have felt as though everybody was constantly, relentlessly screaming at him. The third day we repeated the longeing and ground driving and proceeded to saddling and preparing to mount.

Before getting on, I looked at the saddle and determined that it didn't fit the horse very well, which could have been causing some of the trouble the owner had when he rode him. We talked about ways to make the saddle fit better and tried a different saddle pad that allowed the horse better movement under saddle. The owner mounted up and had what he said was the best ride he'd ever had on the stallion.

On the last day, the owner had an entirely different horse than the one he brought to the clinic. He took the stallion out of the holding pen, without the use of a chain over the horse's nose, and led him quietly along the same route the horse had had so much trouble with only three days before. In the round pen, the stallion stood quietly with his head down and waited patiently to be saddled. The owner got on and proceeded to ride around.

By this time, the stallion had relaxed so much that the look of his body had actually changed. On the first day, he'd been one big ball of rippling, tense muscle, and every step looked uncomfortable. On this last day, his body was relaxed and supple, and he would have almost floated across the ground as he moved, except for one thing. Now that he was relaxed and loosened up, it was clear that he was physically uncomfortable. He was stiff in both hips, his lower back, and one shoulder. In short, he was sore from being ridden.

After about thirty-five minutes, much of which had been at a nice easy trot, the soreness seemed to be getting the best of the stallion. From the fence I told the owner that, even though our time wasn't officially up, it might be best to think about getting off. The owner agreed and said he was just going to trot past the gate and around to the opposite side of the pen and get off.

They were moving past me, headed for the other side of the pen, when the stallion suddenly stopped. The muscles in his face tightened, his nostrils flared, and he shook his head hard—something we hadn't seen from him in two days. I urged the owner to remain quiet and not respond (an easy request to make for someone sitting on a fence thirty feet away). The stallion shook his head a second time and suddenly offered to rear. Again I urged the owner not to respond, and much to his credit, he refrained.

The stallion did rear, but it was only about six inches off the ground. He immediately came back down and stood with a somewhat surprised look on his face for a couple of seconds. Then, very slowly and thoughtfully, the big horse just quietly lay down. On the way to the ground, the owner had time to get off, and he did. The horse laid on the ground for a second or two, climbed back to his feet, and stood softly, with his head down, beside his owner.

To me it was amazing effort on the horse's part to communicate something specific without harming himself or anyone else. It was clear he was very uncomfortable being ridden and needed the rider off his back. But instead of pitching a fit, perhaps throwing his rider or hurting someone, he made a conscious decision not to. Not only that, but he figured out a way to accomplish his goal of getting the rider off in a manner that kept the door open for positive communication in the future.

There were those at the clinic that day who swore the stallion was just looking for a way to avoid work, that in the future the horse would see laying down as a way to get a rider off, that no horse could actually communicate at that level. And quite frankly, I can't prove them wrong. But what if they are wrong? What if horses, along with other animals, are trying as hard as they can to find a way to communicate with us in a positive way, but because we're so stuck on seeing ourselves as "superior" beings, or because we have to feel our theories are right, we don't even give them a chance? Well, for me, it seems that would be one serious lost opportunity. And I guess that's an opportunity I'm not willing to let get past me.

I FEEL PRETTY STRONGLY that Buck spent fifteen years of his life trying to show me the possibilities that are available when we try to find common ground, whether it's between him and me, him and other horses, me and other horses, or me and other people. There is always common ground if we just look hard enough. Once we find it, the doors of communication swing open and the understanding can begin.

When it gets right down to it, a little understanding never hurt anyone.

Practice

PRACTICE MAKES PERFECT, so the old saying goes. Along the way, someone added a word, making it, *perfect* practice makes perfect. I'd like to add to it one more time, making it something like, perfect practice of the *exact thing* you want to make perfect, makes perfect.

An acquaintance of mine, a dancer, tells a story about being in a chorus line. One day the choreographer came in with a new routine. He showed it to the dancers, who practiced it with him a time or two before he was called away to a meeting. In his absence the girls were to keep practicing the series of new steps. They were professionals and very diligent in their practice habits, and each of them strove for perfection. By the time the choreographer returned some forty-five minutes later, the routine was nearly perfect.

With one exception. Somewhere in the middle of the routine, the girls had missed two steps. Even though what they'd practiced was indeed nearly perfect, it was also incorrect.

So the saying, practice makes perfect, doesn't really fit. Even the revised edition, perfect practice makes perfect, doesn't work. If only they'd practiced perfectly the exact thing they wanted to make perfect . . . well, you get the idea. The point I'm trying to make is it's not enough just to practice something we want to get better at. We need to know exactly *what* and even exactly *how* we are going to practice before we get started.

At some point I made a decision to improve myself, not just with horses, but in all aspects of my life, using the lessons I learned from Buck. Early on I remember thinking that for me to get better at those things, all I'd need to do was apply them to working with horses, and everything would just fall into place.

So off I went, working with horses using the six lessons I gleaned from Buck. In every situation I tried hard to be *non-confrontational* and always have a *plan* before entering a pen with a horse. I always tried to be as *patient* as I could, while being *consistent* and *persistent*. And last, but not least, if I had a setback of any kind, I always tried to learn from it, shrug it off, and *move on*.

But while I was working hard at practicing the lessons with my horses, I allowed the rest of my life to go along pretty much like it always had. For instance, if I got into some kind of confrontation with someone, it often ended with no resolution and both of us walking away upset. I constantly struggled with making any kind of plan. I could think ahead, but planning ahead didn't seem all that important. I still had very little patience with employees who did substandard work or made mistakes I thought shouldn't have been made. My kids sometimes received the brunt of my impatience just for doing some sort of "kid thing." And don't even get me started on how I sometimes responded to other people's poor driving habits.

I was persistent and consistent only when I thought there might be some immediate benefit, never giving any thought to long-term consequences, good or bad. And when it came to a personal setback of any kind, I really wasn't doing very well, whether it was with a horse's training, a problem with an employee or a client, or an unresolved disagreement with anybody.

So, as you can see, while I continued to work diligently to use the lessons to better my work with horses, I wasn't applying them in other aspects of my life. Not surprisingly, I wasn't making much improvement. What I failed to understand about the lessons was that my teacher, Buck, didn't turn them on and off when he felt like it. They were a full-time part of him. They made up who he was and how he lived, all the time.

It was only when I came to this realization that things began to turn around for me. My mistake had been that I really wasn't practicing the exact thing I wanted to make perfect.

PRACTICING HAS ALWAYS BEEN something I've enjoyed. I grew up in a family of athletes, so we were always practicing some kind of sport. I was not what you'd call a natural athlete, but I still enjoyed sports. I loved playing basketball, for instance, but I wasn't a very good shot. I figured out early that if I was going to be an asset to a team, I'd need at least one good shot I could make consistently to help put points on the board. I decided on the hook shot, a relatively high-percentage shot that is difficult for opponents to defend.

I can remember practicing the hook shot for hours on end, from every conceivable angle and distance and with either hand. I worked on it during our regular team practice, and I'd stay after practice and work on it some more. I'd work on it during pick-up games with my friends and by myself at the hoop in the driveway. I got so good at the hook shot that it almost always went in, and opponents six inches taller than I could never block it.

When I was about thirteen, I began playing drums on a professional level. I later switched to guitar, which I still play professionally today. From early on, sports practice was interspersed with rehearsals for whatever band I happened to be playing in at the time. When it came to music, again, I wasn't what you'd call a natural. I enjoyed playing, and after buying a set of drums and teaching myself how to play, I spent hours practicing the same roll until it was perfect. A friend (who played bass and also practiced endlessly) and I played together for hours at a time and ended up playing in some of the top bands in the area. It was all because of the way we practiced, and the amount of time we spent practicing.

It wasn't long before I realized practicing the lessons I learned from Buck would be much different than anything I'd ever practiced before. In a sport or with music, the more I practiced, the better I got. It was that simple, and improvement was easy to measure. The more times I took the hook shot, the less I missed. The more I played a rhythm on the drums, the smoother and tighter it got. But this . . . this was much different. Not only was there nothing tangible to practice, but there didn't seem to be any way to measure progress even if I *could* find the thing to practice.

HORSEMANSHIP CLINICS are great places for people to learn and practice. Not only can they learn about their horses and how to work with them, but if they give themselves a chance, they can also learn more about what's going on in their own lives. This kind of learning isn't reserved for the students of the clinic; more times than not it gives the clinicians a chance to grow as well, assuming they can get out of their own way long enough to pay attention to what's happening around them. That's the dilemma I found myself in.

There I was, trying to find effective ways to improve myself and the work I was doing, using the lessons I learned from Buck, but I was having trouble because I couldn't find a starting place. I'd been looking at the lessons as six separate things, each needing its own individual attention. I thought I could take *consistency* and spend one whole day working just on that. Then the next day I would work on *patience*, and then *persistence*, and so on.

During my clinics I began to see there was a different way to look at the situation. I constantly preached two things, in some form or another, to nearly everybody who came to ride with me in a clinic. I urged people to find a way not to fight with their horses and urged them to be clear with their intentions, so the horses could learn exactly what it was they were trying to teach. *Don't fight; be clear* was the message.

Following what had been a difficult clinic where I repeated the mantra, *don't fight; be clear*, to just about everyone who came into the pen, I loaded my horses and began the long trip home. About half an hour later, I found myself traveling through rush-hour traffic in one of the biggest cities in the country. I was in the second of five lanes, and cars and trucks flew past, weaving in and out in front of me, forcing me to hit my brakes unexpectedly, which tossed my horses around inside the trailer. It was obvious I was going to be in the traffic for a while, but after only a few minutes, I could feel my patience to begin to run thin.

A little green sports car zoomed passed me, hit the brakes, pulled directly into my lane, and hit the brakes again. There was no room to stop or avoid hitting him, so I braced my hands on the wheel and stepped firmly on the brake pedal to lessen the blow that was sure to come. At the very last second, he pulled into the right lane and out of my way, barely making it between a UPS truck and long white limousine.

I could feel the horses scrambling around in the trailer as I released the brake pedal and fell back into the flow of traffic. I felt my blood run cold with anger as I watched the driver of the green car hit the brakes again and then accelerate to the right, swerving onto an off-ramp and disappearing into the crowded city streets.

I turned my focus back to the packed highway, every muscle in my body tense, when, out of the blue, I heard my own voice say out loud, "Don't fight; be clear." I'd been telling people that very thing all weekend. I'd said it so many times the words seemed to come out of my mouth automatically.

I said it again, "Don't fight; be clear." I felt myself take a deep breath and loosen my white-knuckle grip on the steering wheel. *Don't fight; be clear*. I checked my mirrors and assessed the traffic behind me. *Don't fight; be clear*. I looked at the traffic in front of me. I took another deep breath and let it out.

I thought of something else I'd said endless times during clinics. Don't let the situation control you; take control of the situation and think while you do it. *Time to slow this deal down*, I thought to myself.

I flipped on my right turn signal to change to a slower lane. Car after car passed me on the right, the drivers ignoring my request for a lane change. *Don't fight; be clear*. I gradually began to creep into the right lane, as if asking if I could merge. Two more cars passed before one slowed and gave me a headlight blink, signaling I could merge in front of him. I guided my rig into the lane, flashed my lights as a thank you, and slowed to a more manageable speed. Just like that, the situation was back under control and my patience was restored, not to mention my feelings of goodwill toward other drivers, especially the polite one behind me.

It was another five or six miles down the road before a huge light bulb came on for me. In one small situation, armed with a simple phrase, *Don't fight; be clear*, I had just practiced all six of the lessons! By not letting the *setback* get control of me, I'd quickly been able to *plan ahead* to get into a slower lane. I'd *patiently* waited for my lane change, and when it didn't come, I asked to move into the lane in a *non-confrontational* way. Through *consistency* and *persistence*, I finally found someone willing to let me merge. I did, and the rest of the drive through town was relatively trouble-free.

My goodness. Surely, it couldn't be that easy. But it was. All six lessons could be practiced simply by using the idea of *don't fight; be clear*, something I'd been preaching to horse people for years. I suddenly felt like Dorothy in *The Wizard of Oz*, who, after everything she'd gone through, found out she could have gone home any time by simply clicking her heels together. The answer to her dilemma had been right under her nose all along, just as mine had. ONCE I BEGAN APPLYING that one simple concept to all aspects of my life, things started to change for me. It seems strange now that I'd thought I needed to practice Buck's lessons separately, picking the situations or the lesson I would work on during a given day.

What I realized was every day is filled with opportunities for me to not fight and be clear. Some opportunities are major and possibly even life altering, others are very small and seemingly insignificant. Even so, each one is equally important in helping me practice my lessons.

I remember one of my teachers in high school telling the class, as we neared graduation day, "In life you will be faced with an endless barrage of uphill battles. Some of these battles will need to be fought, some won't. Remember to always choose your battles; never let them choose you." At the time the words went right past me, and yet, I never forgot them. It was only when I started down the road of *don't fight; be clear* that the words rushed back to me.

For me, picking my battles meant I needed to find ways to set myself up for success in my daily routine. It started with simple things, like conversations. If I happened to be in a conversation where I didn't agree with the ideas being discussed, I'd asked myself if it was really important for me to express my point of view. Did I stand a chance of being heard or would it simply be a waste of time?

Because I looked at my conversations this way, I found myself really slowing down and thinking before I spoke. I gave questions much more deliberate thought. I was able to provide clearer answers that helped people gain the understanding they were looking for more quickly.

This hesitation produced an interesting side effect. Other people would jump in and answer the questions before I could reply. In the past this sort of interruption might have upset me, but with a don't-fight attitude, I began to see that, in the big picture, what I had to say might not be all that important to them.

Now some people might look at this as a defeatist attitude, but I don't see it that way. Not getting the chance to offer my opinion didn't cause me to give up my opinion, it just meant others didn't get to hear it. And in the end, it doesn't really matter to me if my opinion gets heard or not. It's just an opinion, after all.

By participating in conversations with this mindset, the door opened for me to gain more understanding of the other person's point of view. By listening instead of speaking, I gained a broader perspective on the many different lifestyles, ideas, ideals, and backgrounds of the people I was meeting. This, in turn, gave me a better understanding for people I had yet to meet, which often made that critical first meeting go more smoothly. This proved invaluable to me when I went into a new place for a clinic and met new riders and horse owners who were coming to me for help for the first time.

When I started trying to handle situations using *don't fight; be clear*, I slowly began to understand the don't-fight part can be used in many ways. It can mean don't fight with the person you're talking to, don't fight with your horse, don't fight the situation you're in, and even, don't fight with yourself. It was this last one that I found the most helpful overall in my life.

A good example of this, for me, is standing in lines. As long as I can remember, I've hated standing in lines. I think it comes from my days in Catholic grade school where we had to stand in straight lines all the time. Whether we were going to lunch, getting our coats, going to Mass, sharpening our #2 pencils, going to the restroom, or getting ready to be dismissed for the day, standing in line was the rule of the day. (My wife, however, says it's just because I'm not a very patient person.) At any rate, I've never been good at standing in lines, but this, too, began to change.

I realized part of my problem with lines was I was always getting into them when I hadn't planned to. Or, maybe I should say, when I hadn't planned, period. For instance, I'd stop at a fast-food place at lunchtime, when everybody else in the world was stopping for lunch. Just like that, I was in a long line, starving to death, with the five people in front of me all ordering some exotic concoction that didn't even exist on the menu. I'd begin thinking how hungry I was, how inconsiderate those people were being, how I should have come in sooner, how I should have come later, how much I still had to do that day, and how standing in that line was making me late.

Now I realize that I was fighting with myself for not planning ahead better in the first place and for not being patient. So, I started planning better, stopping before eleven in the morning for lunch or before five for dinner, thus avoiding the long lines. If I happened to run into a line anyway, I just looked at it as an opportunity to work on patience. I found that while the lines were slowing my day down, in many cases, my day needed a little slowing down. I was missing a lot by not living in the moment, even if that moment was standing in a line with twenty other people. Suddenly I could hear the friendly conversations of people around me, the occasional joke being told, or the different accents in people's voices—all things I'd missed in the past. I began to see there's a little bit of good even in the things I thought were bad.

Getting stuck in a line at the movie wasn't a bad thing, it was an opportunity! So was being interrupted in a conversation, getting cut off in traffic, and having kids do kid things. Especially the latter, where we get to observe the wonder of youth, smiling faces, learning curves, and fun at large!

I BEGAN TO UNDERSTAND it wasn't Buck's lessons that I needed to be practicing, after all. The lessons are very important, and I greatly rely on them in my daily routine. They're the foundation for the path I want to be on. But what I came to understand, once I began to think in terms of *don't fight; be clear*, is that I was practicing *life*, and those lessons are just part of it. What's more, I was practicing the kind of life I wanted mine to be, whether it was driving down the road, pushing a wheelbarrow, opening a gate, meeting someone for the first time, petting a dog, or riding a horse. Just like that, I was practicing perfectly the exact thing I wanted to make perfect.

Of course, my life and how I would like it to ultimately be is far from being perfect on any level. But then, that does give me something to practice.

The Beginner

———————————

THERE WE STOOD, three of us, barefoot on the carpeted floor of the dojo, beginners in our very first Aikido class. The Shihan—a very high-level instructor in this Japanese martial art that relies on softness, balance, timing, and blending with an attacker—patiently began walking us through the basics of the kata, a series of moves that held the key to everything we would learn. I was forty-six years old and entering into a sport so foreign to me I might as well have been trying to fly the space shuttle.

The stance was very uncomfortable. My right foot was a short distance in front of me and turned at an angle to the outside; my left foot was slightly behind me, also turned to the outside. The majority of my weight was to be supported only by the ball of my right foot, just behind the big toe. My arms and hands were suspended in front of me, the right hand about chest high, and the left about belt high, with my thumbs up and fingers relaxed and pointed forward. The idea was that, from here, power would flow like water from my fingertips.

From this extremely awkward, out-of-balance position, the Shihan had me move forward, backward, and to the side, sliding my feet along the floor and moving my hands and arms in graceful movements that would someday produce power, balance, and speed. That first night I struggled to find a spot in the stance where I wouldn't fall over, never mind achieving perfect balance, speed, and power. After watching me struggle for what seemed like an eternity, the Shihan came over. He placed his hand on my shoulder and said quietly, "It'll come. Don't worry so much about form or getting it exactly right for now. Just do the best you can. Breathe and try to stay soft. Remember you're just a beginner. It's your first time trying this, and your body won't want to do these things. But it will, once it understands what you want."

He smiled, patted my shoulder softly, and went on to the next student. Three things in that one simple interaction had a profound impact on me. The first was the softness this master used to make his point. Here was a man of tremendous agility, speed, and most of all, power, and yet the pat on my shoulder felt like little more than the weight of a bird landing. With all the power at his disposal, he chose a gentle, encouraging touch. The sign of someone who knows true power is always displayed in the softness he offers another.

The second was the fact that, while it was painfully clear to him, as well as everyone who walked into the dojo that night, that I was a rank beginner, he still treated me with the same respect and dignity that he showed the black belts in the class. It had been a long time since I'd been a beginner at anything. While it's a great place to be, with open doors and endless possibilities for growth, it is also a terribly fragile place to be. It doesn't take much for a beginner to find a way to quit, especially if he doesn't get some kind of encouragement that helps him make progress.

It's human nature, I suppose, but when I went into the dojo that first night, I assumed I was going to be good at Aikido right from the start. When I began to realize I wasn't going to be good right away, I started to push myself in an attempt to be as good as I had thought I'd be. Of course, that didn't work. I simply didn't have the knowledge or the skills. The Shihan recognized that and slowly guided me down the road I was on, as opposed to the one I thought I was on.

Finally, and perhaps most importantly, the way the Shihan expressed himself to me, he not only made clear that he didn't expect perfection (or anything close) from me that night, but he also gave me permission to make mistakes. From there on out, that permission became the vehicle for my learning the art.

When I first met Buck, I just assumed, as I had with so many other horses I'd worked with over the years, that he would see me as the teacher and recognize his role as dutiful student. And at the beginning, that was the case, as I taught him how to accept a rider on his back. He worked hard to understand how to give to pressure from the bit, my leg, and even my seat. He learned how to move forward, backward, and sideways on cue, and he learned how to adjust his speed.

It seems that after he had a clear understanding of all those things, I somehow ceased to be the teacher. Our roles ever-so-slowly reversed. I was about to go down the same road I traveled when I started Aikido. I was a rank beginner with a kind and wise master as teacher.

As with that first class of Aikido, my biggest problem was that I didn't recognize I was a beginner. Once you get to a certain age, you assume there won't be much new coming your way, so the chances of finding yourself a beginner at something seem pretty slim. Unlike Aikido, an argument could be made that I wasn't a beginner at horsemanship since I'd been involved with it for so long.

Yet, even after about twenty years of working with horses, what I was about to experience with Buck was still something brand spankin' new to me. Those twenty years of horse work, I decided, were really equivalent to one year of experience repeated nineteen times. I was about to head into uncharted territory.

IN THE YEARS WE WORKED TOGETHER, I only remember a handful of times I used what I'd call force on Buck. The first time was up in the valley when we were trying to cut off the herd. Another time, a colt was giving us problems, and I wanted Buck to move but he refused.

The last time was one morning up at the ranch. I'd gone out into the pasture, a large wooded area where the horses had rested during the night, to bring them in. As we did every morning, Buck and I rode out and made a big circle through the trees until we found the seventy head of horses. They were all standing near the fence, clear up at the top of the hill, nearly as far from the gate as they could get.

Just as we closed in on them, Buck suddenly jumped to one side, landing right on one of the geldings. This spooked the whole herd and sent the horses stampeding through the woods and down toward the gate. Buck took off with them, running as fast as he could under trees, through bushes, and over rocks. My attempts to get him pulled up failed, until we'd traveled a good two hundred yards down the hill. There I finally got his head turned enough to get him stopped.

Unfortunately I let my emotions get the better of me. I swung him around very quickly several times, kicking him in the sides as we went. Then I pulled him around the other way at a high rate of speed. After we stopped, I grabbed the reins much harder than I needed to and pulled him backward for a good thirty feet. About then I saw, out of the corner of my eye, a mountain lion up in the clearing we'd just come through. It was running back up the hill toward the place the herd had been standing only minutes before.

Buck, ears alert but standing stock still beneath me, also watched as the lion disappeared into the trees. We sat quietly for a few seconds. Then I asked him to walk toward the gate about a hundred yards away. He did so without hesitation and without urgency. Here he had probably just saved us from an attack, and my response was to punish him for running off. To top it off, he took my foolish outburst without a fight and went right back to work.

While there really weren't many times I used force on Buck, I can see that they were generally unnecessary. Yet, Buck never seemed to hold a grudge or get upset with me in return, and that was somewhat of a mystery to me. My occasional idiotic outbursts never got much of a rise from him. He would take whatever I dished out and, when it was over, act as if it never happened and simply go back to the business at hand.

His seemingly indifferent behavior caused two changes in me. The first was that I quit using force on him, either in cueing him or as a punishment. If he didn't respond to a cue, I found a way to help him without forcing him. If he offered some unwanted behavior, I first looked for the reason and then sought a way around it.

It took me a while to understand that Buck truly was a great horse. He *wanted* to work with me, so if ever a time came when he offered behavior such as spooking or running away, there had to be a reason. It was almost always a very good reason—something I needed to pay attention to.

The second change was that I began to wonder why he didn't seem too bothered when I lost my mind, flew off the handle, and punished him by using force. I'd used what *I* would refer to as force to "punish" horses in the past, and almost always the horse would exhibit a sort of low-level fear, not wanting *that* to happen again. It was never a feeling I wanted the horses to have, but at the time, I just didn't have the skills or the experience to know how to do anything different to correct unwanted behavior.

Perhaps my lack of skills was why Buck seemed so indifferent to my use of force. I began to wonder if he somehow knew that I didn't know any better. Yeah, yeah, I know that very thought opens up a whole new can of worms. Realistically it would indicate that I was either dealing with an entirely new, unheard-of level of communication between Buck and myself, or that I had simply "gone 'round the bend" for even considering the idea in the first place.

Now before you decide, I should probably explain the reason I thought Buck might view me as a beginner. It's due to some very interesting similarities between these episodes and something else I'd seen him do.

As YOU KNOW, Buck lived in herds of horses all his life, mostly with geldings and mares, but there was the occasional foal, weanling, or yearling, and of course, two-, three- and four-year-olds. The behavior he exhibited with these younger horses may be the key to why he didn't respond in a negative way when I used force with him.

In numerous incidents with the younger horses in the herd, I saw Buck allow himself to be crashed into, run over, run under, gnawed on, and kicked at. Most horses would have put a stop to that behavior pretty fast, usually when a baby got to be about a year old. But not Buck.

Buck allowed this baby stuff to go on until the youngsters got a little older, about three years old. If a youngster that old tried to encroach on his space, he very quickly and decisively put it in its place and the breach would almost never occur again. And yet, up until that age, he was willing to put up with just about any antics and, in most cases, worked to shape the young horse's behavior in some positive way.

For instance, if a colt was particularly frisky with him there were times when Buck would stop to play with him; other times the colt would get absolutely no reaction from him. When Buck played with the colt, the antics might last for quite a while, fifteen to thirty minutes. When he wouldn't play with the colt, the baby would very quickly, usually within a matter of seconds, go looking for someone else to play with. In effect, Buck had taught the colt—a beginner with virtually no experience at being a member of the herd—that there were times when playing with him was acceptable and other times when it wasn't, and he'd done it in a positive way.

With these colts, Buck wasn't just saying, *No, don't play with me!* In my opinion, he was showing them how to differentiate between playful behavior and non-playful behavior in an adult. When he was playing, he *really* played. When he wasn't, he *really* wasn't. The colts could see and feel the difference in him, because there was such a striking contrast between the two behaviors. He was so clear in those behaviors that the colts figured out when they could get him to play and when they weren't going to get a rise out of him no matter what they did. Buck had shaped, in a positive way, what other horses in the herd often looked at as negative behavior from the babies. He had helped them grow.

When I looked at the way Buck treated me on many occasions and how he responded to my use of force, there are a number of striking similarities to his behavior with the babies. For instance, when the colts tried to play with him when he didn't want to play, he outwardly shut down, in effect saying, *I'm not playing today. You need to go look for someone else to play with.*

When I'd ask Buck to do something he thought was inappropriate, particularly when there was another horse involved, he showed basically the same type of behavior. He was probably saying to me, *This isn't going to work very well. You need to look for another way to do this.*

Early on I didn't realize he was trying to help me, so I would thump on him to get him to respond to my requests. Or after he'd responded and the situation blew up, I sometimes punished him for it.

With the babies in the herd, he often put up with all kinds of abuse from them without ever responding, particularly if they were very young, or even if they were a little older but still immature. He treated each horse he was "training" as an individual and tailored his behavior and teaching methods accordingly. If a youngster, no matter how old, was struggling to understand what Buck was trying to present, he was patient with them and they'd eventually catch on.

After stepping back and looking at the situation Buck and I were in, I could see he was doing much the same thing with me. The babies needed to learn about being a proper horse. I needed to learn about being a proper horseman. And while it was clear he didn't care much for substandard behavior from either the babies or myself, he wasn't particularly interested in getting into an argument over it. His non-confrontational approach won out.

Like my experience learning Aikido, before Buck could help me, I had to realize I was a beginner in *his* world. Only when I did this was I able to become open enough to actually learn from him.

By remaining non-confrontational even when I didn't, Buck took the fight right out of me. I finally realized that when Buck was apparently ignoring my outbursts of force, what he was really expressing was, *Well, go ahead and do that if you need to. I realize you don't know any better. I'm sure one day you will, so keep trying.*

Once the fight *was* gone and I no longer wanted to use force of any kind on him, I began looking for ways to better communicate on a number of levels. This, in turn, opened the door to a whole new level of learning and understanding, and it was the catalyst that allowed me to finally see the lessons he was presenting.

The thing that completely amazed me about Buck, and still does to this day, was his ability to accept things with grace, whether it was new information I was presenting, the playfulness of the babies around him, or a forceful and many times uncalled-for encounter with me. Part of it was his ability to give without taking anything in return. That, in and of itself, has humbled me no end.

Now I can look back on all the things I've learned from Buck and see that, like the Aikido Shihan, he was a master teacher well versed in his lessons. It's clear, at least to me, that Buck undoubtedly saw me as a beginner at horsemanship. Yet, he not only didn't hold it against me, he forgave me my indiscretions and proceeded to help me become better at what I do.

I feel very strongly that ol' Buck truly wanted to help me become a better horseman, and a better person, for that matter. To that end he was helping me right up until our very last ride together by giving me the encouragement that helped me progress in the right direction.

I'm sure he would have liked to see me get a little farther down the road before it was time for us to quit, but unfortunately, perhaps for both of us, we simply ran out of time.

PART THREE

Buck's Legacy

One Last Ride

_____

I THINK ABOUT BUCK A LOT these days. To say I miss working with him would be a gross understatement. You see, I've come to the realization that, over all those years we worked together, I depended on him much more than he ever depended on me.

In my mind's eye I can still see us riding quietly together down the mountain trails near our home or chasing a herd of horses through the hills at top speed. I remember moving cattle slowly across the river and my kids sitting in the saddle when they were babies. These pictures, all of Buck in his prime, are interspersed with images of a much older Buck. A wise and kind old horse, friend and teacher, standing in our backyard in his later years, ribs beginning to show slightly, gray hair flecking the areas around his eyes, but happily munching on his ever-present pile of hay.

SOMETIME BACK, Kim, a friend who knew my sons and I were practicing Aikido, gave us a book written by Aikido master Gozo Shioda. The book is full of photos of this small, slightly balding Japanese man in his sixties, a soft and serene look on his face, effortlessly tossing numerous attackers here and there, using the simple idea of blending with an opponent's attack and utilizing timing, speed, and balance to redirect his or her energy. The idea behind Aikido, whether you're the one doing the throw or the one being thrown, is that both attacker and defender walk away unharmed, having both learned something in a positive way from the interaction.

For me, there is a direct correlation between this idea of remaining calm in the face of adversity, blending with a situation, and directing it to a positive outcome, and the way Buck conducted himself, whether with people or with other horses. I can't begin to count the number of times I was witness to Buck's calming influence on a herd of horses, and when it came to interactions with people, his list of accomplishments was equally impressive.

Like the Aikido master, Buck was able to slip in and out of nearly any situation with people—even ones he'd never been in before—with ease and confidence. To Buck's credit, when the situation was over, the person almost always looked and felt better than when he or she began.

A FEW YEARS AGO, the local rodeo queen's horse was injured, and she needed a replacement at the last minute. Buck had never performed the duties of a rodeo queen's horse before, one of which was carrying the queen at top speed around the arena while carrying a four-by-eight-foot flag. Behind the rodeo queen, also riding at top speed, would be the winner of the previous event. Both would gallop around the arena while the crowd, some five thousand people, cheered.

Up to that point, Buck had spent the majority of his days doing ranch work up in the mountains, and with the exception of an occasional parade, he'd hardly ever been to town. He had never carried a flag of any size before, never mind one as big as a sheet of plywood, and he had certainly never seen five thousand people in one place, shouting, cheering, and clapping as if they'd all lost their minds. He went into the situation with minimal preparation on how to carry a flag and no preparation at all for facing that many people. Yet, he stepped up, and during five rodeos over three days, he simply became the rodeo queen's horse. He never faltered or wavered; he did his job and kept her safe until her injured horse had recovered and could go back to work.

The following year, the same rodeo queen, riding a new horse she'd gotten to replace her aging gelding, had a terrible wreck during the first rodeo she rode him in. She had taken the big, black gelding into the arena at top speed, carrying the flag. Just before turning to go through the gate to leave the arena following the run, one of her reins broke, and the gelding careened out of control. He swerved suddenly, tossing the queen and sending her crashing into one of the uprights of the announcer's booth. She ended up with cracked ribs, a broken wrist, and quite a few bumps and bruises.

Because this rodeo—as well as the next five she was supposed to ride in—was held in her hometown, which she was representing as queen, she desperately didn't want the accident to keep her from continuing. But with her injuries, she also wasn't ready to ride the new and still unfamiliar horse she'd just had the wreck on. So Buck stepped in again.

For those next five rodeos, Buck carried the queen—at a much slower, more reserved, safer pace than he had the year before. They circled the arena to the thunderous applause of the hometown crowd, given in appreciation of the queen's bravery and willingness to continue her duties despite her injuries. Under her was the horse that made her presence possible. And even though I doubt Buck would have cared one way or another, I, for one, was hoping at least some of that heartfelt applause was for him.

It was about 10:30 on a moonlit night in August when the phone rang. On the other end was a Rocky Mountain National Park ranger.

"We've got a woman up near Longs Peak," the voice on the other end said in a businesslike fashion. "Hurt her knee on the way down this afternoon and only got as far as the Boulder Field. She's stuck up there above timberline, near Chasm Lake. Can you go up and get her out?"

Longs Peak is the tallest mountain in Rocky Mountain National Park, at over fourteen thousand feet in elevation. It's a popular destination for recreational hikers as well as hard-core mountain climbers. The main route up is a relatively easy climb for most of the way, but it does get tricky near the top. In this area, a place known as The Trough, injuries to climbers often take place. Apparently, this is where the woman twisted her knee. She was with three other climbers at the time, and together her companions brought her down as far as they could. The woman was in a tent on the saddle of a ridge near a place called Jim's Grove. It would be a four-hour trek one way from the trailhead by horseback—and Buck was the horse I would take.

Buck and I reached the trailhead about an hour later, and in the dark I unloaded him and tied him to the trailer. I put on his saddle and bridled him, tied saddle bags with various provisions and a first-aid kit to the back of the saddle, and put on my chaps, heavy jacket, and gloves. I attached a miner's-type headlamp to my hat to illuminate the trail as we made our ascent. I made a quick stop at the ranger station to double-check the woman's whereabouts. I mounted up, and together, Buck and I began the long ride through the dark forest and up the trail.

At first, the thought of a ride in the moonlight through a forest in Rocky Mountain National Park might sound like a wonderful thing to do with your horse. And it is. Providing, of course, you're on a horse that doesn't worry too much about things most horses would. Things such as the shadowy figures of deer and elk as they crash through the trees and bushes in front of you, behind you, and at your sides, the howl of a coyote, or the scream of a mountain lion off in the distance. Not to mention the other nighttime travelers on the trail.

During our trek up the mountain that night, Buck and I occasionally passed hikers out for a moonlight walk, carrying flashlights and walking sticks. We also passed climbers carrying large backpacks and wearing headlamps like the one I had, as they tried to get an early jump on their assault of Longs Peak.

Anyone who has ever done any trail riding and has unexpectedly encountered a hiker wearing a backpack can tell you just how exciting it can be, particularly if their horse has never seen such a sight. Now, think how exciting it might get if you ran into the same thing while riding at night! But Buck never wavered at any of our encounters that night, even though I'd never prepared him in any way to accept the strange sights and sounds we came upon. He simply followed my instructions and walked unperturbed up the trail.

After a few hours we crossed a narrow stream, rounded a bend in the trail, and emerged from the trees. At well over ten thousand feet, we were higher up the mountain than the trees can grow. We were bathed in the bright light of the full moon. In fact, the light from the moon at that elevation was so bright I no longer needed my headlamp.

We traveled a little farther up the trail along a rise and started up a ridge. We topped the ridge and, as you'd expect at that elevation, walked right into a sustained fifty-mile-per-hour wind that nearly knocked Buck off his feet. We continued on for about another half-hour, until we came to a small tent pitched on the highest point of a rock saddle above Chasm Lake. Inside was the injured woman and one of her hiking companions, who had stayed to keep her company and help keep her warm.

The wind-whipped, wildly flapping tent would have been enough to spook most horses, but once again Buck remained calm and stayed committed to his job. After a time, we were able to get the woman out of the tent and mounted on Buck's back. With me leading him, we turned and started back down the trail we'd just come up.

We had barely gotten below timberline when the woman began complaining about how uncomfortable the saddle was. Not how much her knee hurt or how much pain she was in, but how much the saddle hurt her butt! The trail was very uneven and rocky, but Buck slowly and with great care picked his footing as best he could in the dark, while passing hikers carrying backpacks and others stopped on the side of the trail with their maps unfolded and flapping in the wind—all things that would have sent most horses stampeding terrified into the woods, even in the daylight.

"This horse is too bumpy," she whined.

"Can't he go any faster?"

"Why is he so slow?"

"My butt hurts."

"What time is it?"

"Why is he so bumpy?"

Normal conversation with the woman was impossible thanks to all the complaining she was doing. What's worse, as we got farther down the trail, it became clear that she wasn't hurt that much, after all. She had both feet in the stirrups, and there were times when Buck had to take a long step off a water bar, jarring her. But she didn't even flinch. Instead she complained about how the saddle was hurting her butt!

It took us nearly two hours to come back down the trail that had taken us more than twice that long to get up. We'd passed countless things that should have scared Buck, but he never took a wrong step. About a mile from the trailhead, the woman's ranting about her sore butt and Buck's inability to give her a BMW-type ride finally got the better of me.

"Why does this horse have to walk so roughly?" she whined, one too many times.

I stopped Buck and walked back to the saddle. Reaching up, I asked her to climb down.

"What?" she was surprised at my request. "Why should I get down? We're not back yet!"

"It's not far now and the sun is coming up," I told her. "You've been unhappy with my horse since you got on him. I just figured you'd rather walk than ride."

She was quiet for several seconds before saying, "No. I'm sorry. I'd rather ride. He's a good horse."

He's a good horse. Heck, by all rights he should have spooked and run off about fifty times during the trip up and back. He could have easily unloaded her with one wrong step. In fact, there were several times when he actually stepped underneath her when she lost her balance, so she wouldn't come off! She was inadvertently kicking him in the sides pretty much the entire trip, which might have sent other horses trotting or even loping away. He's a good horse? She had no idea.

DURING BUCK'S TIME with me, he did so many great things for me and other folks lucky enough to have ridden him, that it's difficult to catalog them all. In his younger years, he taught hundreds of kids and adults how to ride, including my own kids (and me, for that matter). In fact, at one time or another, he carried everyone from six-year-old children to movie actors and professional football players. He was used as a hunting and packing horse, a parade horse, a guide horse, and an overall ranch horse. He's worked cattle and horses, been roped off of, and even raced a time or two. I've used him to pony colts and older horses from time to time, and he's saved me from other horses more than once.

On one such occasion, we were in a large pen with another horse and rider. The other horse was pretty upset and acting up. The rider was doing a great job of keeping the horse under control and directing him in a positive way, but unfortunately, it wasn't helping the gelding's attitude much. Buck and I were standing quietly nearby, and as was his custom when nothing was being asked of him, he showed little interest in the goings on between the other horse and rider. The gelding was about six feet from Buck and me, and as I coached the rider from Buck's back, the horse suddenly lunged for me, teeth bared, ears pinned, the whites of his eyes showing.

I had no time to react to the charge and watched helplessly as the horse's teeth headed for my right thigh. Again, like the Aikido master in that book, Buck took quiet control of the situation. Without any big move or change in his demeanor, he shifted his weight from one foot to another and took about a half step toward the advancing horse. This half step, less than six inches worth of movement on his part, turned his body just enough that when the attacking horse made contact, his teeth met the back of my saddle, on the skirt right behind the cantle.

Had Buck moved more than six inches, the horse would have hit his hindquarters. Any less and the horse would have bit my leg. As it was, the horse hit the solid leather of the saddle, leaving an imprint of his upper teeth that is still there to this day. The gelding, apparently shocked at meeting such a hard surface, flew backward in surprise. He regained his composure and finally settled down and began to pay attention to his rider's requests.

ON COUNTLESS OCCASIONS, Buck seemed to respond to my thoughts. Sometimes when we were riding, I would begin to think about a change of speed. Without the slightest cue on my part, he would change to the speed I was thinking about. This also happened when I wanted to change direction. Often if I thought about going somewhere, he would just go.

At other times I'd be in the house thinking about going for a ride to check the herd or look the fence over. Buck would be grazing way out in the pasture somewhere, but by the time I'd go to get him he'd be right next to the barn. In our later years on the road together, I'd be walking around or sitting in my trailer, thinking about checking on him. Even before I got near his pen, I'd often hear him nicker softly. Then I'd walk around the corner of the barn to see him looking intently right at me, as if he'd been waiting for me all along.

His apparent ability to read people's minds wasn't always reserved for me, though. A few years ago I traveled with Buck to Los Angeles to film our first video. For two days straight we filmed a variety of horse-and-rider tasks. Because we weren't sure exactly what we'd be filming over the two days, we waited until the end to film the introduction, where I'd talk about the video's contents.

The camera crew began setting up the shot for the introduction. I was to be standing in one spot while Buck, saddled and ready to go, stood behind me. The director placed Buck and me where he wanted us for the shot and began setting up the camera. He placed reflectors so that the sun would illuminate my face and filters so it wouldn't illuminate my face too much, and did a variety of other things, including setting up cue cards. The entire time this was going on, maybe ten minutes, Buck stood behind me, eyes almost closed, apparently sleeping. From the time the setup began, he had not moved a muscle.

With everything finally in place, we were ready to begin filming. The cameraman, not quite satisfied with what he was seeing through his lens, looked up at me with a slightly concerned look on his face.

"Could you get that horse to . . . ," he began.

Before he could finish, Buck, who hadn't moved in ten minutes, raised his head slightly, took one step forward, lowered his head, and went back into rest mode.

" . . . take one step forward," the cameraman continued, his voice tapering off in disbelief.

There were several people standing nearby who witnessed what had just happened. Almost in unison they let out a chorus of "No way!"

"Welcome to my world," I said with a smile. "He does that all the time. Weird, eh?"

Each winter we put most of our horse herd, including Buck, out on pasture. I liked having him there because twice each winter I'd go out and gather the horses so we could trim their feet and worm them. With Buck there, I always knew I had a horse I could depend on for the gather. No matter what, I could always go out, catch him up, toss a saddle on him, and go straight to work. No muss, no fuss.

This day started out no different than the hundreds of other times I'd used him for a gather of one kind or another. I caught him up without a problem, and we got underway just as we always had. We quickly gathered the herd and drove them to the far end of the pasture where the catch pen waited, gate standing open. Everything was going along just as smoothly as it always did, when suddenly one of the new horses, a young gelding we'd recently bought at a sale, panicked, turned away from the herd, and bolted.

Before the youngster got completely turned, Buck and I were headed at a full gallop in the direction he was thinking about going. The colt ran hard some thirty feet away from the west fence line, heading north, away from the herd and the catch pen. With the angle we were taking and the speed that Bucked possessed, I was pretty confident we'd have him turned in a matter of seconds.

We got out ahead of him and met him at a spot along the fence about a hundred yards from the herd. The youngster hit the brakes hard and turned back. I asked Buck to stop and cut back as we'd done thousands of times, but this time, he couldn't. It was obvious that he was trying to get the cut put together, but he just couldn't get his legs under him in time. Instead of responding, he plowed forward helplessly, nearly running into an irrigation ditch. By the time we reached the ditch, he had slowed enough for me to ask for a turn. Oddly enough, it was as if his steering had gone out as well. He continued to plow forward, turning slowly as he went. He finally got turned back, just in time for us to see the youngster running past the catch pen at full speed, taking the rest of the herd with him. They ran clear to the other end of the pasture.

Buck tried hard to catch them, but it was as if he'd suddenly burned up that enormous engine of his. That effortless speed, the endless stamina that he had always possessed, even a few months before, was suddenly gone. For the next hour or so, we worked at a much slower pace and eventually got the herd gathered again. But from that day forward, Buck was never the same.

In all the time I'd ridden Buck, he hadn't missed a cut while gathering either horses or cattle. Even if an animal was lucky enough to get past him, it was never past him for long. With his speed and agility, Buck usually caught the renegade within a few strides and brought him back to where he needed to be. Missing the cut that day seemed to be hard on Buck mentally, more than physically, and he seemed very depressed for the rest of that day. He still did the work, but it was definitely without the passion and sense of fun he usually had.

OVER THE NEXT COUPLE OF YEARS, Buck struggled off and on with minor health problems. They were never anything serious, but they nagged him. For instance, even though his teeth were in good shape and were looked after by an equine dentist, and although he was wormed on a regular basis and given only high-quality feed, he still had trouble keeping weight on. At one point he developed a cough, which we controlled with an antihistamine after we found he was sensitive to dust in his feed—something that had never troubled him before.

He was intermittently uncomfortable physically, as well. I upped the chiropractic adjustments he was getting, kept his feet trimmed and shod, and generally began giving him more special care. I also got him a saddle that fit him even better than the one I'd used for the past thirteen years.

All of this seemed to help, but I worried about him a lot for another year before I finally realized what was going on. It was something I never really expected and never prepared for—Buck was simply getting old.

In the following year, Buck came up lame in his front end from time to time. I had him looked at by farriers, vets, chiropractors, and message therapists without finding a concrete reason for the lameness. So for that entire year, I struggled with keeping him sound. I rode him every other day at clinics and sometimes only half days at that. I kept him on "Bute," a painkiller, when he was uncomfortable, and continued to search for a reason for the lameness. That year I seriously began to consider retirement for him. He was twenty-one years old.

During our time off that winter, December and most of January, I made the decision that the coming year, 2000, would most likely be his last year on the road with me, barring any major improvement. It was an eventuality I truly dreaded. Much to my surprise, that year Buck showed a marked improvement in both his attitude and his physical ability. It was almost as if, once again, he knew what I was thinking, and he stepped right up and gave me one of the best years we'd experienced in a while. With the exception of the intermittent lameness, he stayed sound and kept his weight on pretty well. He seemed genuinely happy to go to work each day. At the end of November, as we closed out that year, I put Buck on winter pasture with high hopes for the coming year.

The 2001 season started out with a long road trip to Texas in February. We did a couple of clinics in southern Texas, then one near Austin, before heading to Ft. Worth to ride in the benefit for the master horseman, Tom Dorrance. I'd been invited to ride in the benefit months before and had been looking forward to riding Buck in the horsemanship part of the program. By the time we got to Ft. Worth, however, we had been three weeks nonstop on the road, and Buck was very tired. His lameness seemed to hover right under the surface. It wasn't noticeable yet, but it wasn't far away, either.

On the way to the benefit, I made the decision to ride Smokey, who was along on that trip. I'd started riding him in December, getting him ready to go on the road that year as my relief ride when Buck couldn't work. He was green, but pretty solid, and beside, I figured it'd be good experience for him.

That plan fell apart as soon as I reached Ft. Worth. A fellow clinician who had been invited to the benefit wasn't able to bring a horse and asked if she could use one of mine. At first I was reluctant, but in the end, I gave her Smokey to ride. I felt confident that he would do a good job for her, and even though I wanted to give Buck the weekend off, I figured I'd ride him knowing that I'd just pull out of the class if it was too much for him.

The morning of the benefit Buck and Smokey were in good spirits. About an hour before the class, we saddled them up and took them to the warm-up arena. Along with several other riders, we walked, trotted, loped, and did a few stops. For the remaining warm-up time, we mostly just rode around and visited. Buck was tired but sound, and I felt pretty confident he'd be okay during the class.

Still, as we lined up to enter the arena, I told myself in no uncertain terms that on that day, nothing would be more important to me than my horse. No matter how many people were watching the class, no matter what task we were asked to do, no matter what, Buck would come first.

We rode into the arena with about forty other riders and joined the swirling mass of horses and riders, as we all traveled clockwise on the rail with some eleven-hundred people looking on. Buck was solid as a rock, even when horses next to him suddenly flew apart. Occasionally he would look around to check on Smokey's whereabouts, but other than that, you'd have thought he was going for a stroll on one of the trails near the ranch.

I had never ridden with or even seen Ray Hunt before, the master horseman and author who was conducting the horsemanship class, so I had no idea what to expect or what to do, for that matter. My feeling of being somewhat lost wasn't helped by the fact that, from inside the arena, the P.A. system was difficult to hear. With the help of some quiet coaching from clinician Lee Smith, who had fallen in behind us, Buck and I finally got headed in the right direction and were on our way.

Over the next hour and a half, Ray asked us to do a number of tasks as a group: walk, trot, lope, stop, turn on the haunches, turn on the forehand, and then do the same in the other direction. Ray said several times that he wanted us to do these things without troubling our horse, and that became my main focus. Our transitions weren't as fast as they could have been, but Buck wasn't troubled. We could have stopped much better than we did, but Buck wasn't troubled. Our turns weren't very quick, but they were relatively clean, and Buck was okay with them. Often during the class, Buck and I were the last ones to complete the task that had been given, but I felt good about the fact that we were doing it together, as a team.

About two-thirds of the way through the class, I felt Buck's energy start to go, but he still gave me everything he had. When the class was over, Ray asked us all to line up so that he could make a few introductions of the riders. While the others rode to the line-up area, I dismounted, loosened the cinch, and led Buck to a spot near the rail where we were to stand. He had given me what he could during the class, and I saw no point in using him for a chair during the rest of it.

We stood in line while the introductions took place, each rider going to the center of the arena as his or her name was called. I stood with Buck at my shoulder and, somewhere in a quiet part of my mind, made the conscious decision that his would be Buck's last year on the road with me. No sooner had that thought crossed my mind than I felt a gentle nudging at my right elbow. It was Buck, eyes half closed, leaning his head on my arm. I reached over and stroked his forehead, and for just that fleeting moment, he and I were the only ones in the building.

That year, 2001, turned out to be a great one for us. About two months after the benefit, we discovered the reason for Buck's intermittent lameness, which turned out to be some bruising on his heels. With some special shoeing, the problem all but disappeared, and he was sound for the remainder of the season. He was suddenly able to keep weight on, and because of that, he seemed to perk up considerably.

Even with Buck's soundness and health issues apparently resolved, I was still committed to retiring him at the end of the year. To that end, I made a point at every clinic to announce his retirement. That way, I knew I wouldn't be able to back out of it.

During that last year, as much as I hate to admit it, I began to realize that I'd come to rely on Buck almost too much. We had become such close partners that cues were almost nonexistent and were often not needed. Jobs we did had become easy to the point of complacency on my part. And I believe it was because of that complacency that I was perhaps falling below my potential as a rider and a horseman. I knew it, and I think he knew it, too. Great teachers all know that at some point, they need to move their students on to the next level, whatever that happens to be. And as much as I hated to see it come, apparently it was our time.

THE LAST CLINIC OF THE YEAR was held in Texas, not far from where we started the season. It was hosted by a couple of friends who knew about Buck's retirement, and one night during the clinic they gave an impromptu retirement party for him, complete with carrot cake. Buck was great during the clinic, where we did arena work and trail work, and where, for one last time, he and I worked a colt together. He also did some wonderful demonstrations of collection, half pass, and passage, all usually performed by upper-level dressage horses, not twenty-three-year-old ranch horses.

I had planned on giving Buck the last day of the clinic off. The last day was going to be mostly trail riding, and Smokey needed the trail work much more than Buck. But then one of the clinic participants, a woman who was working a colt not yet ready for the trail, expressed an interest in going on the trail ride with us and asked if she could borrow a horse from someone. At the last minute, I offered Buck.

As always, Buck was rock solid out on the trail. When the ride was over, we were all gathered in the arena sitting on our horses, going over what we'd done during the ride. The woman on Buck casually mentioned how easy he had been to ride.

"I didn't really have to do anything," she said in amazement. "He definitely knows his job."

It was an understatement. As we sat there in the arena, me on Smokey, the new kid on the block, and Buck with yet one more student on his back, I couldn't help but see the aptness of the situation. How fitting for Buck's last working ride to be not with me on his back, but with someone who was a perfect stranger to him, someone just starting down the path that he'd been trying to help me down for years.

I realized then how far down that path I still had to travel. But instead of feeling overwhelmed, I actually felt lucky. Heck, I was still a beginner! And as a beginner, all doors and all possibilities are open. Could it be that this is what Buck was trying to say to me all this time? Was he saying to me, *Rejoice in where you're at, don't worry about where you aren't?* Well, if it was, after fourteen years and thousands of hours together and almost as many rides, standing there in that arena in Texas, I finally got it.

THESE DAYS BUCK STANDS in our backyard, happily enjoying his retirement. From time to time he takes our ten-year-old son, Aaron, for rides around the area, but other than that his days are pretty quiet.

The other day I was standing at the window looking at him while he munched away on his morning ration of hay. I was getting ready to start writing down my thoughts for this book and was having trouble thinking of a place to begin. I was thinking of how great an impact this horse has had on my life and how important true communication is, whether between people or between animals and people. I was hoping I'd find a way to get that point across without sounding sappy or ridiculous.

About then, Buck slowly raised his head from the pile of hay and looked directly at me. His mouth was full, but he wasn't chewing. His ears were up, his eyes bright and knowing, and we both stood looking at each other. Within seconds my anxiety about the whole thing just vanished. It was as if I'd called a former teacher to help me with a problem I couldn't solve myself. Suddenly, out of nowhere, I had this feeling as if someone, somewhere was saying to me, *Just do the best you can . . . The rest will take care of itself.*

And so I will.

Afterword

Buck passed away quietly in the very early hours of New Years Day, 2004. He had a heavy winter coat, plenty of feed and water, and he hadn't been sick. It had been a cold night but not unseasonably so, and certainly not any colder than Buck had been accustomed to. I had gotten the sense in the months leading up to his passing that Buck was beginning to feel his age, which at the time was twenty-four years old, but even with that he had been in relative good health. When I found him that morning, there were no signs of struggle as one might find if a horse had died from some internal or external ailment.

I mention all of this because in the years since his passing, I have gone over all of these things countless times in my mind. Many was the night that I lay awake and wondered whether there might have been something I could or should have done that would have kept him with me for one more year or month or day. But even after all that soul-searching and sleepless nights, I finally came to the understanding that there really wasn't anything I could have or should have done or that I missed. It had simply been Buck's time to move on, and that was that.

Buck and I had been nearly inseparable for the seventeen years we were together. We worked colts and cattle, gathered horses, been on thousands of miles of trails, did mountain search and rescues, and traveled coast to coast countless times. He even taught all three of my kids and numerous other adults and children how to ride. He was a kind soul, a patient teacher, and a once-in-a-lifetime partner that I find myself thinking about every day—and who I miss very much.

In the weeks and months following Buck's death, I found myself dogged by a state of mind that I later came to realize I was ill-equipped to deal with. This period of grief and sadness was like nothing I had ever felt before, and to say it was an unfamiliar place to be would be an understatement. Up until then I had always found that my responses to most situations, regardless of severity, urgency or importance, all fell into the same category, one of reserved neutrality.

This emotional neutrality stemmed from the fact that all throughout my life I had spent a great deal of time working on ways to stay emotionally balanced and cognitive even during the most stressful of situations. And emotionally balanced was what I had become—or at least so it seemed.

However, in the years prior to Buck's death I found myself wondering about the normalcy of my responses and reactions to certain "serious" situations. For instance, when I attended the separate funerals of two close friends who had both been killed in accidents, I was certainly saddened by their loss, but the grief I felt didn't approach the grief that others there seemed to be going through. Of course I realize everybody responds differently to death, but even so, when I looked back on other funerals of friends or family, I became aware of a very similar pattern in my emotional response: brief sadness followed by relative indifference.

Over time I began to realize that this indifference had become my natural response to most situations and in particular ones that others might find troubling, sad, urgent, serious, or—even on the other end of the spectrum—joyous. It made me wonder why my response was so dramatically different from what others seemed to be experiencing. Were other folks were over-reacting or, on the other hand, did I under-react? Because my responses had always been the same for as far back as I could remember, I really had no way of knowing if they were normal or not. All I knew was that they were normal for me.

Then Buck died, and suddenly everything changed. For the first time in my life I found myself experiencing raw emotions that I had seen in other people but never felt myself. I assumed at the time that the wave of indifference that had always come over me following similar situations would eventually show up, but it never did. In fact, not only did the rawness of what I felt that day linger for months, but, more importantly, something else occurred that shed some light on why I had always experienced such an apparent lack of emotion during similar situations.

During the weeks and months immediately following Buck's death, I found myself experiencing vague but disturbing childhood memories. Without my going into details, it will suffice to say that these were memories of very specific traumatic events I had long since buried deep in my subconscious and that over time I had just assumed were gone for good. The memories began slowly, with one showing up just a few days after we had buried Buck. Within a week, however, I was experiencing these memories nearly every day, and then over time, every day, and sometimes several times a day. The more frequent the memories occurred, the more vivid and realistic they became. I even began waking up in the middle of the night drenched in sweat after experiencing one or more event in the form of extremely lucid and frightening nightmares.

I didn't know it at the time, but for many years I had actually been suffering the severe effects of Post Traumatic Stress Disorder (PTSD). One such symptom, I would later learn, was the indifference I experienced during times of what would have normally been some sort of emotional discomfort. When I became overly sad or stressed, a defense mechanism known as disassociation would kick in, causing me to become almost completely devoid of emotion until the situation passed.

Regardless of the cause, this bottling up of emotion is not good for the body or the soul. Eventually, when the body has had enough, it will do whatever it needs to do to make things right. All it takes is the right trigger to get the ball rolling. For me, that trigger was losing Buck. Not only did his passing open up the door to emotions long ago closed off, but it also began the process of purging my system of the traumas I had experienced as a child. That purging began in the form of the memories that I seemingly had no control over.

Those memories, which started as nothing more than vague childhood reminiscences in the days following Buck's death, eventually turned into full-blown and uncontrollable flashbacks that came on at the most inopportune times. Some of these flashbacks would be so real it was as if I was reliving the trauma all over again, and often they would actually be temporarily debilitating. Many was the time I had to stop whatever I was doing or saying and take a minute to reorient myself back to the conversation or task at hand once the flashback had passed.

For the next three years this pattern of flashbacks, disorientation, and then reorientation occurred with such frequency and intensity that I decided my only hope at getting any relief was to seek some help. Even with that, however, in the weeks and months that followed, things went from bad to worse. Along with the flashbacks, I started experiencing occasional panic attacks. And not only had I never experienced such things before or knew what they were or how to deal with them, but it seemed as though they would come on for no apparent reason. Just like the flashbacks, the panic attacks were almost impossible to stop once they started.

In the spring of 2007, however, and just as I was beginning to think things were never going to get any better, my situation reached critical mass. It happened at a clinic I was doing up in the Northwest. I had not been eating very well leading up to that particular trip, having lost over twenty-five pounds in the previous two months, and I had only been getting about two to three hours of sleep per night. In fact, on the way to that particular venue, I didn't sleep at all, having driven the truck and trailer twenty-six hours straight with only one brief rest stop to get the horses out of the trailer for a break.

I remember very little of what happened at the clinic. I do recall working the first day, but don't remember anything of the people, horses, or what we did with them. I remember there was some sort of trigger that caused me to break down, but don't recall what the trigger was. I remember asking the host to cancel the remainder of the clinic after that first day and my leaving the venue the next day, but I don't remember driving.

The next thing I do remember clearly was that I was in the desert south of Moab, Utah, where my horses and I spent the next three days. That "down" time away from people and responsibilities was apparently all that was needed to right the ship because by the time I finally headed back toward home, the hurricane-like storm that had been going on in my mind for the past three years had all but disappeared. Gone were the panic attacks and nightmares, and the flashbacks that had been so debilitating just a few days earlier had lost not only lost their intensity but their frequency. Over the next several months they dissipated into nothing more than the vague recollections of a long ago past.

I eventually came to understand that, as painful as my condition had been, what I had gone through is actually commonplace in cases similar to mine. My flashbacks, nightmares, and vivid memories were simply a way for my subconscious to bring the events I had experienced was unequipped to deal with as a child to the forefront so that I might deal with them in a productive manner now as an adult.

The good news was that even though I still had some work to do before I could make a full recovery (and in fact, am still working on it), the really difficult part was over. But even as I was finally able to look forward as I began healing from the events of my childhood, for the first time in my life I was also able to take an honest look back and see the effects that those long ago events had on my past. The behavior I had always assumed was 'normal' or just part of my personality was actually my subconscious finding ways to hide how I actually felt.

For years through even my early fifties, I had been extremely mindful and even hyper-vigilant about being wronged by others. As a result, I lived in what some might refer to as a low level state of paranoia, often being quick to make decisions based on whether or not I thought someone was trying to "pull one over" or otherwise harm or otherwise hurt me. Along with this response, I had also become somewhat withdrawn and found it very awkward to be around or even carry on conversations with people I didn't know.

Some of my behavior became impulsive, compulsive and self-destructive, such as drinking too much. Often was the time over the years I purposely and needlessly inserted myself into unsafe situations even though I knew the potential for physical injury was very high. Many was the time I paid the price for making such a decision. All of this and other similar behavior took their toll on me and on personal relationships with friends and family. Unfortunately, I ultimately alienated some friends and eventually even my wife, who, having suffered through all of this for the nearly twenty years that we were married, asked for a divorce.

Losing Buck seemed to hit some sort of reset button in me. Suddenly I had an overwhelming need to want to shake off the past and begin anew, and once the process had started, it was clear there would be no going back.

Today, I feel as though I have stepped through a heavy screen in which on one side everything was black and white, and on the other everything was in color. I can now see very clearly all the time I wasted in my relationships with family and friends. As a result, all of these relationships hold so much more meaning to me now than they ever had. The compulsive and harmful behavior I exhibited has all but disappeared, and in its place is a healthier and more thoughtful lifestyle, which includes (among other things) regular daily exercise, much healthier eating habits, and a better balance between work and rest.

I am now remarried to a wonderful woman who helps me find the good in all things—including myself—and who reminds me in her own way to take each day as it comes regardless of the circumstances the day brings. My entire life is much quieter, purposeful, and meaningful, and the ghosts of the past are just that . . . ghosts. The only difference is that now those ghosts have no teeth, no power, and no place in my life.

When I wrote this book about Buck, I wanted to share with the reader some of the important things I had learned from him during our time together. In looking back now, nearly ten years later, I can honestly say that the single most important thing I learned from him was something I received only after he was gone. Losing Buck taught me that none of us are here forever, and that the time we do have is actually very short in the big scheme of things. We all have choices to make when it comes to what we do with the time we have here. We can choose to wall ourselves off or get bogged down in the past, as I had for many years, or we can choose to embrace the life we have been given and become a viable part of it as it moves us forward.

There is no question that Buck's death was the single saddest and most painful thing I had ever gone through in my life up to that point. However, I can also see that it was his death that ultimately gave me something a lot of people in this world never get: a second chance at living the life they always wanted to live.

Of all the things that Buck provided for me over the years, and of all of those things for which I am thankful, I think it goes without saying that it is this second chance at life that holds the most meaning to me. I can also say with unbridled certainty that it is an opportunity that I won't be squandering any time soon.

MARK RASHID

2011

About the Authors

Mark Rashid is an internationally acclaimed horse trainer known for his ability to assess situations from a horse's point of view. He has been working with horses since he was ten, and he was especially lucky in his youth to meet a wise "old man" (Walter Pruitt) who taught him to use communication, not force, in working with horses. Ever since, he has committed himself to finding the quiet but effective ways to resolve even the most difficult problems with horses.

Rashid gives dozens of clinics each year, as well as private lessons. His clinic format of one-on-one work with horse and rider is immensely popular and has gained him legions of fans around the world. In addition to his clinics, Rashid has presented at the National American Humane Horse Abuse Investigators School, the Colorado Horse Fair, and Equitana USA. He has also been a guest on NPR's *The Horse Show*, and he's been featured on the

Nature series on PBS. He is the author of three previous books, *Considering the Horse, A Good Horse Is Never a Bad Color*, and *Horses Never Lie: The Heart of Passive Leadership*. His articles have appeared in *Western Horseman* and *Western Horse* magazines, as well as other publications. He lives in Estes Park, Colorado.

Harry Whitney (foreword) prefers not to call himself a *horse trainer*. Instead, he's simply someone who sees things from the horse's point of view; someone fluent in the language of horses. A perceptive, kind, and clear instructor, Whitney is able to help folks understand their horses—not only for their benefit, but for the benefit of their horses.

Harry Whitney has been featured in *Equus* magazine, *The Whole Horse Journal*, and other publications. His clinics have the enthusiastic recommendation of a wide variety of professionals in the horse industry, including people involved in cutters, reiners, paso finos, Peruvians, foxtrotters, Arabians, quarter horses, endurance, dressage, and therapeutic riding.